UNIVERSITY OF MEMPHIS LIBRARIES
3 2109 00584 2696

MAIN LIBRA
DATE DUE
11-22-01

D0208548

DISCHARGED
DATE DUE

THE FAILURE OF GOTHIC

THE FAILURE OF GOTHIC

Problems of Disjunction in an Eighteenth-century Literary Form

ELIZABETH R. NAPIER

CLARENDON PRESS · OXFORD

1987

Oxford University Press, Walton Street, Oxford OX2 6DP
Oxford New York Toronto
Delhi Bombay Calcutta Madras Karachi
Petaling Jaya Singapore Hong Kong Tokyo
Nairobi Dar es Salaam Cape Town
Melbourne Auckland
and associated companies in
Beirut Berlin Ibadan Nicosia

Oxford is a trade mark of Oxford University Press

Published in the United States
by Oxford University Press, New York

British Library Cataloguing in Publication Data
Napier, Elizabeth R.
The failure of Gothic: problems
of disjunction in an eighteenth-century literary form.
1. English fiction—18th century—History and criticism.
2. English fiction—19th century—History and criticism.
3. Gothic revival (Literature)
I. Title
823'.0872 PR830.T3
ISBN 0-19-812860-6

Library of Congress Cataloging in Publication Data
Napier, Elizabeth R., 1950-
The failure of Gothic.
Bibliography: p.
Includes index.
1. English fiction—18th century—History and criticism.
2. Horror Tales, English—History and criticism.
3. Gothic revival (Literature) I. Title.
PR858.T3N37 1986 823'.0872'09 86-16465
ISBN 0-19-812860-6

Set by BH Typesetters & Designers, Oxon
Printed and bound in Great Britain by
Biddles Ltd, Guildford and King's Lynn

To
F.G.R.,
S.S.R.,
and the memory of
E.R.S.

The signora Rosalina has a secret enemy; bid her to beware of—of——

Mary-Anne Radcliffe, *Manfroné; or, The One-Handed Monk* (1809)

One must have taste to be sensible of the beauties of Grecian architecture; one only wants passions to feel Gothic.

Horace Walpole, *Anecdotes of Painting* (1762)

Preface

In 1794, a reviewer of the Gothic tale, *Count Roderic's Castle; or, Gothic Times,* expressed anxiety about 'the present daily increasing rage for novels addressed to the strong passions of wonder and terrour'. 'The class of readers, for whom this kind of entertainment is provided,' he wrote, 'as if no longer capable of deriving pleasure from the gentle and tender sympathies of the heart, require to have their curiosity excited by artificial concealments, their astonishment kept awake by a perpetual succession of wonderful incidents, and their very blood congealed with chilling horrours.'[1] This sense of alarm over a growing, undiscriminating readership for Gothic fiction is registered repeatedly by reviewers of the latter part of the eighteenth century. '[A]lmost all novels', one writer complained, 'are [now] of the terrific cast.'[2] [T]he press groans,' wrote another, 'and our circulating libraries are filled with books, under the title of romances and novels, which are entirely made up of stories of ghosts and spectres.'[3] Commentators on fashionable fiction took disparaging (though often humorous) note of the proliferation of Gothic novels, which swarmed from publishing houses like the Minerva Press in London. The epigraph for one such review divided the blame between Germans and women:

> Grim-visaged heroes, class'd in martial hosts,
> And walking skeletons, and sheeted ghosts,
> Here hold their court, from German fetters free,
> And doom poor common sense to slavery.
> Ye female scribes! who write without a blot,
> 'Mysterious Warnings' of—the Lord knows what;
> O quit this trade, exert your proper skill,
> Resume the needle, and lay down the quill.[4]

[1] *Analytical Review,* xx (1794), 489.

[2] 'Terrorist Novel Writing', *Spirit of the Public Journals,* i (1797), 229.

[3] 'Anti Ghost', 'On the New Method of Inculcating Morality' [Letter to the editor], in *Walker's Hibernian Magazine; or, Compendium of Entertaining Knowledge* (1798), pt. i, p. 11.

[4] 'Modern Literature', *Aberdeen Magazine: or, Universal Repository,* iii (1798), 338.

One critic, writing in 1796, wagered with dismay that the Gothic would supplant the realistic novel in the popular imagination,[5] and a year later, T. J. Mathias confirmed the prediction with evident distaste: '[Walpole's] Otranto Ghosts have propagated their species with unequalled fecundity. The spawn is in every novel shop.'[6]

Though such reviewers (in the interest of reform) may have exaggerated their readers' predilection for Gothic romance, it is obvious that the genre enjoyed a remarkable reception at the close of the eighteenth century. Lists of new publications appearing in the *Monthly Magazine, Edinburgh Review,* and *Library Journal* between 1796 and 1806 suggest that at least one-third of the novels published in Great Britain during that time were 'Gothic in character'[7] and by 1805 the popular *Lady's Magazine* was devoting over three-quarters of its space to short or serialized Gothic fiction.[8]

The prominence of the Gothic coincided, significantly, with a rapid expansion of the reading public in England. The consequences of the decision in 1774 to enforce the Copyright Act of 1709 had been immense: cheap editions of British classics, no longer under perpetual copyright, suddenly became available, and Lackington's second-hand bookshop, book clubs, and the circulating libraries—which had grown steadily in popularity since the 1740s—contributed to swell and 'democratize'[9] a previously limited and élite reading public. Access to books

[5] Review of John Bird, *The Castle of Hardayne; a Romance,* in the *Analytical Review,* xxiii (1796), 55.

[6] *The Pursuits of Literature: A Satirical Poem in Four Dialogues. With Notes,* new edn., rev. and corr. (London, 1797), p. 87 n. iii.

[7] R. D. Mayo, 'Gothic Romance in the Magazines', *PMLA* lxv (1950), 766.

[8] R. D. Mayo, 'How Long Was Gothic Fiction in Vogue?', *Modern Language Notes,* lviii (1943), 61. One measure of the popularity (and adaptability) of Gothic novels was their rapid assimilation into the periodical magazines and miscellanies: translations, excerpts, and serializations appeared, along with some original fiction, as did synopses and pirated or truncated versions of already published works (see Mayo, 'Gothic Romance in the Magazines', 762–89). One short-lived periodical, *The Marvellous Magazine and Compendium of Prodigies* (1802–3), flourishing at the height of the Gothic craze, offered nothing but abridged versions of tales of sensation.

[9] Richard D. Altick's term, *The English Common Reader: A Social History of the Mass Reading Public, 1800–1900* (Chicago, 1957), p. 63. For a useful summary of reading patterns in the eighteenth century, see Altick, 30–66, and I. Watt, *The Rise of the Novel: Studies in Defoe, Richardson and Fielding* (Berkeley and Los Angeles, 1957), pp. 35–59. For statistics that challenge the conventional views of eighteenth-

was, moreover, coupled by increased leisure in which to read them, in particular among women of the middle class.

Gothic fiction—which came into vogue at this period of increasing literacy and leisure—developed its distinctive generic characteristics rapidly. Walpole, in the preface to the second edition of his *Castle of Otranto* (the work that established the general pattern of the genre in 1764), spoke with vigour of the 'novelty of [his] attempt'[10]—'I have composed it in defiance of rules, of critics, and of philosophers,' he would later write to Madame du Deffand,[11]—and discoursed at some length about his daring endeavour to unite ancient and modern romance in a work of the imagination that was distinctly new. His boast that Shakespeare was his model does not conceal the fact that Walpole's main concern is with his inventiveness, with the idea that he has 'created a new species of romance', that he sees as 'original' and 'daring'.[12]

In 1778, Clara Reeve called her *Old English Baron* a 'Gothic Story', and spoke of it as a species 'not new', making clear her indebtedness to Walpole even as she drew important stylistic distinctions between her novel and his:

> This Story is the literary offspring of the Castle of Otranto . . . it is distinguished by the appellation of a Gothic Story, being a picture of Gothic times and manners. . . .
>
> In the course of my observations upon [*The Castle of Otranto*], it seemed to me that it was possible to compose a work upon the same plan, wherein [the] defects [of exaggeration] might be avoided . . .[13]

Though Radcliffe and many other of the more prominent authors of Gothic fiction like Maturin chose to term their works

century libraries as storehouses of fiction and of women as their chief patrons, see P. Kaufman, *The Community Library: A Chapter in English Social History,* Transactions of the American Philosophical Society, NS lvii. vii (1967), and 'In Defense of Fair Readers', *Review of English Literature,* viii (1967), 68–76.

[10] Horace Walpole, *The Castle of Otranto: A Gothic Story,* ed. W. S. Lewis (London, 1969), p. 7.

[11] 'Je l'ai fait en dépit des règles, des critiques, et des philosophes; et il me semble qu'il n'en vaille que mieux' (Walpole to Madame du Deffand, 13 Mar. 1767, no. 55, in *The Yale Edition of Horace Walpole's Correspondence,* ed. W. S. Lewis *et al.* (48 vols., New Haven, 1937–83), iii. 260).

[12] *The Castle of Otranto,* p. 12.

[13] Clara Reeve, *The Old English Baron: A Gothic Story,* ed. J. Trainer (London, 1967), pp. 3–5.

'romances' rather than 'Gothic stories', the conventions of the romantic tale of sensation became clarified quickly enough for critics in the 1780s and 1790s to speak confidently of them as belonging to a distinctive 'class' of fiction. The reviewer of *The Castle of Mowbray. An English Romance* (1788) thus enters the author into 'the lists as the rival of Horace Walpole, and Miss Lee',[14] and William Enfield, in his review of *The Mysteries of Udolpho,* in like manner praises Radcliffe's novel for possessing certain qualities 'in common with many other productions of the same class'.[15] Often, the categories of 'Gothic' or 'romantic' are simply synonyms for 'unoriginal' or 'repetitious'. Sir Walter Scott refers in this way to the 'Radcliffe school' of writers with its predilection for 'banditti, caverns, dungeons, inquisitors, trap-doors, ruins, secret passages, soothsayers, and all the usual accoutrements'. 'We do not dwell upon any of these particulars [of machinery],' he says in a review of Maturin's *Fatal Revenge; or, the Family of Montorio,* 'because the observations which we have to hazard upon this neglected novel apply to a numerous class of the same kind, and because the incidents are such as are to be found in most of them.'[16] Imitation and satire depend, of course, precisely on an accepted canon of conventions, and the Gothic was widely imitated and often (even by its own practitioners) mercilessly burlesqued.[17]

The present work attempts to re-evaluate a mode of fiction that, for at least two decades, took a firm and distinctive (and, as some critics thought, destructive) hold on the popular imagination of eighteenth- and nineteenth-century English

[14] *Critical Review,* lxvi (1788), 577. A reviewer in a later number of the *Critical Review* seeks in a similar way to clarify the characteristics of Radcliffe's *The Romance of the Forest* by citing its resemblance to *The Castle of Otranto* and *The Old English Baron:* 'The greater part of the work resembles, in *manner,* the old English Baron, formed on the model of the Castle of Otranto' (2nd ser., iv (1792), 458).

[15] *Monthly Review,* 2nd ser., xv (1794), 279.

[16] *Quarterly Review,* iii (1810), 345; 344.

[17] See E. Birkhead, *The Tale of Terror: A Study of the Gothic Romance* (London, 1921; repr. New York, 1963), pp. 128–44; A. B. Shepperson, *The Novel in Motley* (Cambridge, Mass., 1936), pp. 154–81; and L. C. May, *Parodies of the Gothic Novel* (New York, 1980). Both Beckford and Lewis engaged in such mock-Gothic efforts. See Beckford's *Modern Novel Writing* and *Azemia,* and many of Lewis's plays, in which the Gothic frequently becomes matter for comedy.

readers. The fact that the Gothic achieves its florescence at an especially significant moment in history leads us to consider it with particular care: reaching its height at the decline of the classical period, the genre could offer a clue to the emergence of a romantic view; because many of its writers (and readers) were women, it might shed light on some aspects of feminine social and literary history that have until recently been neglected; and as a (largely unconscious) response to the Revolution in France, it might reflect some of the political uneasiness of the latter part of the century. The Gothic has, in fact, lately been receiving attention in all of these areas. Critics such as Masao Miyoshi, Elizabeth MacAndrew, and Judith Wilt have stressed the incipient romanticism of the Gothic[18]—a romanticism stemming in particular from the theological and psychological dread that is its predominating characteristic.[19] Feminist readers of the Gothic, like Bette Roberts, Ellen Moers, Sandra Gilbert, Susan Gubar, and Margaret Anne Doody, focusing on the imagery of enclosure and escape that marks the genre, have claimed its pertinence in delineating the distinctively feminine problems of constricted social, sexual, and authorial roles in the period.[20] David Punter and Ronald Paulson (following Sade and Sadleir) have more recently attempted a decoding of Gothic romance in political terms.[21] 'By the time *The Mysteries of Udolpho* appeared (1794),' as Paulson has written, 'the castle,

[18] M. Miyoshi, *The Divided Self: A Perspective on the Literature of the Victorians* (New York, 1969), pp. 3–45; E. MacAndrew, *The Gothic Tradition in Fiction* (New York, 1979); J. Wilt, *Ghosts of the Gothic: Austen, Eliot, & Lawrence* (Princeton, NJ, 1980). Robert Kiely, who examines the romantic features of the Gothic from a different point of view, summarizes the classificatory problems of such an investigation in *The Romantic Novel in England* (Cambridge, Mass., 1972), pp. 1–3.

[19] See, for example, J. Porte, 'In the Hands of an Angry God: Religious Terror in Gothic Fiction', in G. R. Thompson (ed.), *The Gothic Imagination: Essays in Dark Romanticism* (Pullman, Washington, 1974), pp. 42–64.

[20] B. B. Roberts, *The Gothic Romance: Its Appeal to Women Writers and Readers in Late Eighteenth-century England* (New York, 1980); E. Moers, *Literary Women* (New York, 1976), pp. 90–110; S. M. Gilbert and S. Gubar, *The Madwoman in the Attic: The Woman Writer and the Nineteenth-century Literary Imagination* (New Haven, 1979), *passim.*; M. A. Doody, 'Deserts, Ruins and Troubled Waters: Female Dreams in Fiction and the Development of the Gothic Novel', *Genre*, x (1977), 529–72. For an application of such a reading specifically to Ann Radcliffe, see M. Poovey, 'Ideology and *The Mysteries of Udolpho*', *Criticism*, xxi (1979), 307–30.

[21] D. Punter, *The Literature of Terror: A History of Gothic Fictions from 1765 to the Present Day* (London, 1980); R. Paulson, *Representations of Revolution*

prison, tyrant, and sensitive young girl could no longer be presented naively: they had all been . . . sophisticated by the events in France.'[22]

Though each of these approaches to the Gothic offers a helpful perspective on late eighteenth-century romances, an alert reader of Gothic fiction may turn from these criticisms with the feeling that the works have been misread in some fundamental sense, that the experience of reading the Gothic has been misrepresented, and its rewards exaggerated. Since the 1960s, critics have tended to adhere to the notion that Gothic fiction provides a link between a classical age and a romantic one through its exploration of human emotions and dreads. Yet how differently the Gothic deals with these concerns from, for example, Richardson's *Clarissa* (1747–8) has never been carefully established. And in a perverse turn of critical fate, deconstructive commentators on the Gothic (like Jerrold E. Hogle) are now modernly celebrating that very accusation of vacuity that earlier supporters of the genre were reluctant to concede.[23] The range of critical attitudes to the Gothic has obscured a central question of the genre (and the most compelling one for serious readers of eighteenth- and nineteenth-century fiction). It is time to ask how significant are the issues the genre raises and how thoughtful is its commitment to them.

The following study of the Gothic focuses on works written between 1764 and 1820, the dates of publication of Walpole's *Castle of Otranto* and Maturin's *Melmoth the Wanderer* respectively, with a special emphasis on early works of the genre. Such parameters reflect both contemporary judgement and modern convention. Walpole's *Castle of Otranto* was

(1789–1820) (New Haven, 1983); D. A. F., Marquis de Sade, *Idée sur les romans,* ed. O. Uzanne (Paris, 1878); M. Sadleir, *The Northanger Novels: A Footnote to Jane Austen*, English Association Pamphlet no. 68 (November, 1927) (Oxford, 1927). A more recent study combines the psychoanalytical and historical approaches to the Gothic to argue that the genre articulates the search for a selfhood that is culturally defined. See W. P. Day, *In the Circles of Fear and Desire: A Study of Gothic Fantasy* (Chicago, 1985). A more complex and persuasive treatment of this idea appears in D. Cottom, *The Civilized Imagination: A Study of Ann Radcliffe, Jane Austen, and Sir Walter Scott* (Cambridge, 1985).

[22] Paulson, *Representations of Revolution*, p. 221.

[23] J. E. Hogle, 'The Restless Labyrinth: Cryptonymy in the Gothic Novel', *Arizona Quarterly,* xxxvi (1980), 330–58.

systematically referred to as the first Gothic tale, and by 1820, on the publication of *Melmoth,* the *Monthly Review* spoke of Maturin's work as a revival of a mode of fiction decidedly (at least for 'better readers') on the wane:

> The taste for horrors, or for tales abounding in supernatural events and characters, compacts with the devil, and mysterious prolongations of human life, has for some years past been on the decline in England. The necromancers of the Rhine, the Italian assassins of Mrs. Radcliffe, the St. Leons of Mr. Godwin, &c., &c., had indeed begun to disappear, overwhelmed by their own extravagance, previously to any positive symptom of a returning relish for sense and nature . . . yet [the works] still [retain] . . . their station in the first rank of the provincial circulating library . . .
>
> Still, however, it is confessedly *possible* for a man of decided genius to revive, for a while, this exploded predilection for *impossibility*, even among betters readers . . .[24]

As one of the chief aims of this study is to isolate the distinctive stylistic techniques of the Gothic, and hence delimit the genre with greater strictness, I am not centrally concerned with the assessment of Gothic elements in later nineteenth- and twentieth-century fiction. The propriety of employing the term 'Gothic' to describe such works is, in any case, open to question.

[24] Review of *Melmoth the Wanderer,* in the *Monthly Review,* 2nd ser., xciv (1821), 81–2.

Acknowledgements

This study was assisted by generous grants from the Penrose Fund of the American Philosophical Society; the Andrew W. Mellon Foundation, under whose auspices I spent 1983–4 as a Mellon Faculty Fellow in English at Harvard University; the National Endowment for the Humanities; and the Faculty Research Fund of Middlebury College. I am most grateful for the support of these organizations.

The excerpt from Walpole's 'Autograph Diary of Admission to Strawberry Hill, 1784–1796', which appears as the epigraph of Chapter 3, is reprinted by permission of the Houghton Library.

Contents

Introduction

'The horrible and the preternatural', Coleridge wrote in a review of Matthew Lewis's *The Monk*, 'have usually seized on the popular taste, at the rise and decline of literature. Most powerful stimulants, they can never be required except by the torpor of an unawakened, or the languour of an exhausted, appetite.'[1] In failing to meet Coleridge's charge of moral and aesthetic trifling, the recent resurgence of interest in the Gothic has obscured some central, critical problems of a historically important literary genre. It is impossible to read even the major Gothic novels of the period without being uncomfortably aware of the truth of Coleridge's remarks, or of Walpole's flippant assessments of his own influential *Castle of Otranto*, which he repeatedly referred to as a 'trifle'.[2]' 'It was fit for nothing', he wrote to Hannah More, 'but the age in which it was written . . . that required only to be amused'.[3]

Such statements are difficult to reconcile with the prevailing current view of the Gothic as '[venturing] into the dark night of the irrational',[4] a judgement that is reiterated in many critical introductions and recent dissertations on the genre.[5] One of the Gothic's most eloquent and pioneering spokesmen, Robert D. Hume, has praised the genre on precisely these grounds: 'One of [the] most prominent concerns [of the Gothic]', he writes, '. . . might grandiosely be called a psychological interest. As early as Walpole (1764) there is a considerable

[1] *Critical Review*, 2nd ser., xix (1797), 194; repr. in *Coleridge's Miscellaneous Criticism*, ed. T. M. Raysor (London, 1936), p. 370.

[2] See, for example, Walpole to William Mason, 17 Apr. 1765, *Correspondence*, xxviii. 7; Walpole to Sir David Dalrymple, 21 Apr. 1765, *Correspondence*, xv. 105; Walpole to Madame du Deffand, *c.*17 Jan. 1773, *Correspondence*, v. 316.

[3] Walpole to Hannah More, 13 Nov. 1784, *Correspondence*, xxxi. 221.

[4] M. Miyoshi, *The Divided Self: A Perspective on the Literature of the Victorians* (New York, 1969), p. 5.

[5] Most modern writers adopt this assumption without question. See, for example, J. Wilt, *Ghosts of the Gothic: Austen, Eliot, & Lawrence* (Princeton, NJ, 1980). The attempt, perhaps, is to balance the damaging evaluations of earlier works, for example, D. Daiches, *A Critical History of English Literature* (2 vols., London, 1960), ii. 740; J. M. S. Tompkins, *The Popular Novel in England 1770–1800* (London, 1932; repr. Lincoln, Nebraska, 1961), pp. v–vi.

amount of concern for *interior* mental processes'.[6] The Gothic was seldom complimented by its contemporary critics—the most Scott would say of Maturin in his review of *Fatal Revenge* (a novel he clearly admired) was that he should consider turning his talents to other subjects[7]—and before the 1960s evaluations of Gothic fiction tended to be damaging, often in the extreme.[8] In the past fifteen years, this attitude has undergone a radical change. The 'psychological concerns' of the Gothic have become a critical commonplace, and students of the genre have often adopted (perhaps unwittingly) Gothic vocabulary and conventions—and sometimes even style—to dramatize their views. 'Thus the Sleep of Reason', Judith Wilt writes, explaining the Gothic connection to the experience of 'dread',

> bred both the eighteenth-century dream of being shaken in a giant hand and the nineteenth-century dream of being transfixed by the alien eye from within. And in the twentieth century, a simpler age where Reason never sleeps but goes out to conquer day and night, the Gothic needs few mediating dream images but is a straightforward account of counterattacks by invaded foreigners intent on turning us into mindless Bolsheviks or into helpless guinea pigs for their experiments—foreigners with names like Dracula, and Yug-Soggoth, and Pazuzu from Iran, and with no name, like the Body Snatchers, whose pods are even now, in a 1978 film update of this fifties classic, coming out of California on fruit trucks.[9]

This impressionistic type of criticism may give us a sense of how the Gothic *feels* to one sensitive reader, but its casual psychoanalytical and political rhetoric is in the end analytically self-defeating, for it obscures in its enthusiasm the very assumptions it should be examining. Is the Gothic the product of the 'sleep of reason'? Does the early Gothic function chiefly through dreams? Are fear and victimization its overriding concerns? Since the work of Montague Summers in the 1930s, the

[6] R. D. Hume, 'Gothic Versus Romantic: A Revaluation of the Gothic Novel', *PMLA* lxxxiv (1969), 283.

[7] *Quarterly Review*, iii (1810), 347.

[8] Samuel Chew, for example, refers to imitators of Radcliffe and Lewis as producers of works 'into whose noisome fastnesses we need not descend'. See 'The Nineteenth Century and After (1789–1939)', in A. C. Baugh (ed.), *A Literary History of England* (New York, 1948), p. 1196.

[9] Wilt, *Ghosts of the Gothic*, p. 9.

Gothic has attracted this kind of effusive analysis, which celebrates (but never finally considers carefully) the 'profound depths' of Gothic fiction.

Two works on character in the Gothic—Eve Kosofsky Sedgwick's 'The Character in the Veil: Imagery of the Surface in the Gothic Novel' and Coral Ann Howells's *Love, Mystery, and Misery: Feeling in Gothic Fiction*[10]—have recently called this stand into question. Both are concerned not with the psychological complexities of Gothic novels but with the tendency of Gothic writers to emphasize external and superficial manifestations of emotional behaviour over and above inner psychological states. 'Though [Gothic writers]', Coral Ann Howells points out, 'always insist on the powers of feeling and imagination they tend to concentrate on external details of emotional display while leaving readers to deduce for themselves complex inner psychological movements, from such evidence as a "certain wildness of aspect" or a "settled paleness of the countenance."'[11] The result is a strange deadening of character, a deflection of emphasis from 'psychological depths' to physical and physiological surfaces.

This argument over the Gothic's 'psychological interest' perpetuates a tradition of criticism of Gothic fiction that is radically bifurcated—especially on questions of quality.[12] The positions are dramatically enough opposed to merit further attention. One explanation of the differences might be that the Gothic is attempting to render psychological truths that it cannot fully confront but that certain more enlightened critics (adopting, as Sedgwick has pointed out, a Freudian view of the

[10] E. K. Sedgwick, 'The Character in the Veil: Imagery of the Surface in the Gothic Novel', *PMLA* xcvi (1981), 255–70; C. A. Howells, *Love, Mystery, and Misery: Feeling in Gothic Fiction* (London, 1978).

[11] Howells, *Love, Mystery, and Misery*, p. 15.

[12] Detractors of the Gothic have already been listed. Among its enthusiasts (and its standard historians) are E. Birkhead, *The Tale of Terror: A Study of the Gothic Romance* (London, 1921; repr. New York, 1963); M. Lévy, *Le Roman 'gothique' anglais 1764–1824*, Publications de la Faculté des Lettres et Sciences Humaines de Toulouse, sér. A, t. 9 (Toulouse, 1968); E. Railo, *The Haunted Castle: A Study of the Elements of English Romanticism* (London, 1927); M. Summers, *The Gothic Quest: A History of the Gothic Novel* (London, 1938; repr. New York, 1964); D. P. Varma, *The Gothic Flame, Being a History of the Gothic Novel in England: Its Origins, Efflorescence, Disintegration, and Residuary Influences* (London, 1957); and E. MacAndrew, *The Gothic Tradition in Fiction* (New York, 1979).

self 'as depth')[13] have been able to deduce from it. If this is the case, the Gothic has simply been subjected to overreading, an activity that derives from a recurrent desire to find in the Gothic a transitional form that links, through greater emphasis on the human psyche, the classical and the romantic periods. But the relationship of Gothic to romantic is not necessarily a conjunctive one, and our interest in seeing the Gothic as 'pre-romantic' has, perhaps, obscured the possibility that the genre is actually sending out very contradictory impulses about its own intentions, adopting certain strategies to thwart the very perceptions it seems to be on the brink of achieving.

It is my intention in this study to suggest that the imprecision and extremes to which the Gothic has been subjected critically are in part a result of instability and cross-purposes in the form itself, a feature of the Gothic that has not yet received systematic attention. The emphasis, indeed, in contemporary and recent criticism alike, has been on the remarkable coherence of the genre, of the routine likeness of one romance to another.[14] The genre does achieve stability by repeating a certain pattern of accepted conventions but this should not mask the fact that the Gothic, throughout its florescence, is formally and stylistically marked by disequilibrium. Its recurrent concern with moments of scenic imbalance and dissolution and its tendency towards formal unevenness suggest its practitioners' profound uncertainty about both its generic status and its intent. This aspect of the Gothic is apparent in both sophisticated and popular examples of the genre and any serious revaluation of the Gothic must take it into account. The mode's preoccupation with situations of violent oppression and its predilection for settings of physical decay (ruins and partially inhabited castles and cloisters) become, under this scrutiny, though perhaps less than designators of a troubled psyche, more than thematic or scenic gimmicks; they throw into relief tensions and evasions that hint at the Gothic's peculiarly liminal status (both in terms of literary quality and philosophical importance), at its difficult and uneven breaking

[13] Sedgwick, 'The Character in the Veil', 255.

[14] Scott's laments over the 'Radcliffe school' and contemporary objections to the mindless uniformity of the genre are examples of such a response.

away from the more carefully structured and considered narratives of the preceding period. Walpole suggests the potential magnitude of this change in the metaphorical references to obstruction and release in the preface to the second edition of his *Castle of Otranto:* he hopes that his 'new species of romance' will liberate those 'great resources of fancy' that have in modern fiction 'been dammed up, by a strict adherence to common life'.[15] But Walpole's charge is, ultimately, met hesitatingly by Gothic writers. Two opposed, and often battling, currents mark the genre: a tendency towards moral and structural stabilizing characteristic of much previous eighteenth-century fiction, especially marked in early Gothic novels, such as those by Clara Reeve and Ann Radcliffe, and a contrary inclination towards fragmentation, instability, and moral ambivalence, which reaches its height at the end of the period, with the works of Godwin and Shelley. The Gothic novel remains essentially a genre of imbalance, because its authors finally neither ascribed convincingly to either extreme nor found a middle way between them. A state of stability, however desirable it may be structurally, not only often seems incompatible with the social and psychological worlds the Gothic writers attempt to portray; it exhibits, in paralysis and collapse, some strikingly sinister qualities as well. Instability, though it succeeds more fully in engendering the quintessential 'Gothic' mood, poses aesthetic and moral problems that are equally difficult to solve: inadequate, or incomplete, resolution of structure or theme may hint simply at a reluctance on the part of the author to deal conclusively with the ethical and formal issues of his work. Neither mode (nor combination of modes) in the end worked well for the Gothic. The uneasy shuttling between structures did not produce, as it would later,

[15] *The Castle of Otranto: A Gothic Story,* ed. W. S. Lewis (London, 1969), p. 7. Walpole's notion has been taken up by many critics of the Gothic, and informs a central theory of the period. Michel Foucault, for example, argues of the classical era that, in dealing with the insane, it confined 'an enormous reservoir of the fantastic. . . . Even as [the eighteenth-century madhouses] separated reason from unreason on society's surface, they preserved in depth the images where they mingled and exchanged properties' *(Madness and Civilization: A History of Insanity in the Age of Reason,* trans. R. Howard (London, 1967), p. 209). For an application of this dictum to eighteenth-century Gothic fiction, see, among others, M. Byrd, 'The Madhouse, the Whorehouse, and the Convent', *Partisan Review,* xliv (1977), 268–78.

for example, for Wordsworth and Coleridge, those sublime moments of discontinuity in which a 'higher' meaning is sensed or achieved.[16] This is why the denomination of Gothic as romantic in Weiskel's sense of the word is misleading. Moments of discontinuity such as those Wordsworth experiences in the blind beggar passage or in the Simplon Pass section of *The Prelude* lead directly to the sublime because they are buttressed by a whole battery of images and a control of language and perspective that Gothic novels lack. Even the most cursory look at one of these passages (and at Weiskel's analysis of it) makes evident the inapplicability of this kind of analysis to Gothic romance:

When Wordsworth sees the blind beggar in London, it is the epiphany of absolute limitation which precipitates the sublime moment. The beggar wore on his chest 'a written paper, to explain/His story, whence he came, and who he was.'

> Caught by the spectacle my mind turned round
> As with the might of waters; an apt type
> This label seemed of the utmost we can know,
> Both of ourselves and of the universe;
> And, on the shape of that unmoving man,
> His steadfast face and sightless eyes, I gazed,
> As if admonished from another world. (*P[relude]* 7. 641–49)

The beggar is our epitome or type; he represents *our* world, what we can *know* at the point where earthly limits become definitive. But just at this point—which corresponds to the flash when the light of sense goes out—the other, *unknown* world comes into being, like the invisible world of the Simplon Pass passage. We are 'admonished' and placed in an attitude of respect as we feel our incapacity of attaining that 'other' world.[17]

I stress this point in part because many recent critics, lacking Weiskel's astuteness and discrimination, and fascinated by romantic fragmentation, have insisted upon and celebrated its presence in the Gothic, using its occurrence as evidence of the

[16] Thomas Weiskel has perceptively analysed such moments in *The Romantic Sublime: Studies in the Structure and Psychology of Transcendence* (Baltimore, 1976).

[17] Weiskel, *The Romantic Sublime*, p. 44.

genre's 'elevated' form. Though such a diasparactive[18] structure may, indeed, be more profound and 'true' than a balanced and orderly one, it can also be a sign of artistic uncertainty or a simple lack of skill that is not reaching hesitantly for a 'higher' (because less determinate) meaning. It is essential to make such distinctions in the case of the Gothic because of its peculiar likeness to many of the more searching works that it in part inspired. The Gothic does, in fact, exhibit many of the procedures of fragmentation and disjunction that the romantics, as Thomas McFarland has recently pointed out, would elevate to art, but they seldom at this early stage lead to the profound realizations about human consciousness that some critics have asserted that they do. It is with this systematic failure that the present study is concerned.

[18] Thomas McFarland's term, from Greek διασπαρακτός 'torn to pieces', διασπαράσσω 'rend in pieces', *Romanticism and the Forms of Ruin: Wordsworth, Coleridge, and Modalities of Fragmentation* (Princeton, NJ 1981), p. 4 n. 1.

1 *Techniques of Closure and Restraint*

Many Gothic novels, following a pattern made popular in eighteenth-century poetry and prose, exhibit a strong tendency towards closure, towards stabilization and formal resolution. In no other respect does the Gothic novel betray its kinship with previous fiction more clearly. The urge to stabilize, especially marked in the early Gothic, indeed is often so extreme that other facets of the work, such as character and probable plot, are sacrificed to it; the occasionally disjunctive results are rarely acknowledged or explored. (Mary-Anne Radcliffe is a hesitant exception: she concludes *Manfroné,* her sensational tale of evil, with the directive that the reader should attempt to extract from it lessons of virtue and happiness.) That closure should be insisted upon with such vehemence, and often with such *naïveté,* may strike one as surprising in view of the fact that these novels have repeatedly been called 'pre-romantic'. Structurally speaking, few of the early works exhibit designs that are consciously or coherently 'romantic' (at least in McFarland's or Weiskel's sense of the term). This failure to depart in any radical way from the structures of prevailing modes of fiction suggests the essentially conservative attitude of many of the first Gothic writers. Intent, it seems, on adapting to the current taste for the marvellous, or on stretching the limits of fictional design to see, for example, how extreme or remote an experience may still afford a lesson in moral sentiment, the early Gothic remains undisruptive because the basic structure of its experience is still so familiar.[1]

[1] Many Gothic writers, interestingly, professionally preserved this balance between conservatism and novelty by writing both in accepted 'higher' modes and in the Gothic manner. Eliza Parsons, for example, wrote Gothic novels as well as satirical, sentimental, and historical fiction; Clara Reeve wrote both supernatural tales and novels of education; and Walpole wrote widely (indeed, primarily) in other genres.

RESOLUTION AND CLOSURE

The need to solve and resolve (seen most clearly in Ann Radcliffe's desire to explain the supernatural occurrences in her tales) is a striking feature of early Gothic. In *The Castle of Otranto, The Old English Baron, Longsword,* and the novels of Ann Radcliffe, the ultimate aim is a state of moral and social equilibrium. The vicious are punished, the virtuous are rewarded, and social and ethical imbalances are tidily corrected. *The Castle of Otranto* opens with a complex and mysterious tangle of political and familial relationships. Manfred, falsely reigning in Otranto after his grandfather's murder of Alfonso the Good, seeks to ensure the continuation of his princedom by uniting his line with that of the family he has wronged. Unable, finally, to forestall a mysterious prophecy about the loss of the kingdom he has usurped, the villain's plans collapse, and the story ends with the true heir of Alfonso restored and Manfred retired to do penance in a convent. *The Old English Baron* (a story that revolves similarly around a murder and an unjust usurpation) concludes with political and ethical inequities again set to rights: Edmund, the son of the murdered Lord Lovel, assumes his rightful title and marries the virtuous Emma, and Sir Walter, his crimes revealed, is permanently banished from England. Even the haunted apartment undergoes a transformation: it is repaired and refurbished for the use of the faithful Sir Philip Harclay. Leland's *Longsword,* one of the earliest historical novels to exhibit 'Gothic' traits, in an effort to achieve a similar final equilibrium, even goes so far as to defy the historical events on which it is based. The Earl of Salisbury, who in actual fact died from the poison given him by Hubert de Burgh, triumphs over his enemy and lives on in fiction to a ripe and rewarding old age. The management of priorities is particularly interesting here. The demands for historical accuracy (despite the assertions at the opening of the story) are clearly not as strong as those for structural balance and ethical justice. Throughout these works, aesthetic pleasure seems to derive from simple—indeed, simplistic, and often forcible—resolutions of situations of imbalance: identities are confirmed, families reunited, and rightful heirs restored.

In this almost obsessive desire to mete out rewards and punishments at the works' ends, it is not unusual to encounter frequent allusions to a coming resolution: Reeve and Walpole (as, later, Radcliffe and Lewis) utilize prophecies and dreams to prepare the reader for the revelations of character and event that are to come, and both novelists make use of family resemblances (Theodore–Alfonso; Edmund–Lord Lovel) to foreshadow the relationships that lie at the centre of the novels' mysteries. The prediction of such resolutions is a relatively simple affair; it depends mainly, as Sedgwick has argued, upon the reader's ability to recognize superficial similarities among characters and events. In works in which characters are delineated with more subtlety, the achievement of resolution brings more dramatic procedures into play. In such works, sudden tonal shifts or abrupt flattenings of character may occur as the authors make decisions about their players' final destinies. Thus, La Motte, in Ann Radcliffe's *The Romance of the Forest,* whose weaknesses have given rise to a complex combination of sympathy and detestation on the part of the reader, is not permitted to share in the concluding celebration of Adeline and Theodore, despite his apparent reform. The novel's absolute polarization of good and evil necessitates that virtuous and erring characters finally remain permanently apart. Radcliffe's dismissal of La Motte from the novel he has helped to energize suggests the tensions inherent in such a situation:

For La Motte, who had been condemned for the robbery on full evidence, and who had been also charged with the crime which had formerly compelled him to quit Paris, a pardon could not be obtained; but at the earnest supplication of Adeline, and in consideration of the service he had finally rendered her, his sentence was softened from death to banishment. This indulgence, however, would have availed him little, had not the noble generosity of Adeline silenced other prosecutions that were preparing against him, and bestowed on him a sum more than sufficient to support his family in a foreign country. This kindness operated so powerfully upon his heart, which had been betrayed through weakness rather than natural depravity, and awakened so keen a remorse for the injuries he had once meditated against a benefactress so noble, that his former habits became odious to him, and his character gradually recovered the hue which it would probably always have worn, had he never been exposed to the tempting dissipations of Paris.[2]

La Motte, under the pressures of the happy ending that banishes misfortune and vice, virtually ceases at the finale of the novel to function as a character: he becomes, rather (through the subjunctive tense), something he 'might have been', and at last is erased: his response to his fate contributes not to an understanding of his own character, but highlights the charity of Adeline.

Radcliffe's experiments with ethically mixed figures (like La Motte) are usually this cautious. Though in *The Mysteries of Udolpho* there are brief moments that betray an admiration of Montoni, and though in *The Italian* she shows an increased interest in characters of this kind, in the end she is unwilling to confront the complex moral judgements such 'tainted' heroes would demand. As a literary character, Schedoni meets a fate more punishing than La Motte: allowed a generous share of the reader's sympathy as the novel progresses, he is made to sacrifice it at the close as Radcliffe causes him to perform a revenge against Nicola that erases any trace of goodness in his character:

Schedoni's struggles now began to abate, and in a short time he lay motionless. When he unclosed his eyes, death was in them. He was yet nearly insensible; but presently a faint gleam of recollection shot from them, and gradually lighting them up, the character of his soul appeared there; the expression was indeed feeble, but it was true. He moved his lips as if he would have spoken, and looked languidly round the chamber, seemingly in search of some person. At length, he uttered a sound, but he had not yet sufficient command of his muscles, to modulate that sound into a word, till by repeated efforts the name of Nicola became intelligible. At the call, the monk raised his head from the shoulder of the person on whom he had reclined, and turning round, Schedoni, as was evident from the sudden change of expression in his countenance, discovered him; his eyes, as they settled on Nicola seemed to recollect all their wonted fire, and the malignant triumph, lately so prevalent in his physiognomy, again appeared as in the next moment, he pointed to him. His glance seemed suddenly impowered with the destructive fascination attributed to

[2] Ann Radcliffe, *The Romance of the Forest,* new edn. (3 vols., London, 1827; repr. New York, 1974), iii. 278–9.

> that of the basilisk, for while it now met Nicola's, that monk seemed as if transfixed to the spot, and unable to withdraw his eyes from the glare of Schedoni's; in their expression he read the dreadful sentence of his fate, the triumph of revenge and cunning. Struck with this terrible conviction a pallid hue overspread his face; at the same time an involuntary motion convulsed his features, cold trembling seized upon his frame, and, uttering a deep groan, he fell back, and was caught in the arms of the people near him. At the instant of his fall, Schedoni uttered a sound so strange and horrible, so convulsed, yet so loud, so exulting, yet so unlike any human voice, that every person in the chamber, except those who were assisting Nicola, struck with irresistible terror, endeavoured to make their way out of it. . . . The consternation of the Marchese and of Vivaldi, compelled to witness this scene of horror, cannot easily be imagined.[3]

Radcliffe's hesitation at working with 'mixed' characters is seen most complexly in *The Mysteries of Udolpho,* the most openly self-questioning of her novels, in the figures of Valancourt and St Aubert. Both these men, essentially good, are made to appear to err. St Aubert reveals a connection with the Marchioness de Villeroi that is mysterious and possibly romantic, and Valancourt during Emily's absence appears to have involved himself in a life of dissipation in Paris. For modern readers, these aspects of Valancourt's and St Aubert's characters are interesting, for they deepen and considerably humanize the two men. To discover that their supposititious deeds are, in effect, devices to delay the catastrophe of the story and to extend a sense of mystery that is one of plot, not of psychology, brings Radcliffe's priorities startlingly into focus. The issue of Valancourt's offences is settled, summarily, when it is discovered that his lapses have been unjustly exaggerated; the more tantalizing question of St Aubert's guilt, a possibility that Radcliffe keeps open almost to the end of *Udolpho,* is similarly closed when the identity of the Marchioness de Villeroi is revealed. In both of these cases, Radcliffe toys with, but ultimately retreats from, the creation of potentially complicated characters into the realm of moral absolutes.[4]

The finales of many Gothic novels, particularly, underline the authors' special desire to impose stability and meaning

[3] Ann Radcliffe, *The Italian or the Confessional of the Black Penitents: A Romance,* ed. F. Garber (London, 1968), p. 402.

[4] In one respect, of course, her suggestions about St Aubert and Valancourt are

upon the events they have created: 'Here', Radcliffe writes at the end of *A Sicilian Romance,* 'the manuscript annals conclude. In reviewing this story, we perceive a singular and striking instance of moral retribution. We learn, also, that those who do only THAT WHICH IS RIGHT, endure nothing in misfortune but a trial of their virtue, and from trials well endured, derive the surest claim to the protection of heaven.'[5] 'All these [papers], when together,' concludes Reeve in like fashion in *The Old English Baron,* 'furnish a striking lesson to posterity, of the over-ruling hand of Providence, and the certainty of RETRIBUTION.'[6] *The Mysteries of Udolpho* ends on a similarly resonant note: 'O! useful may it be to have shewn, that, though the vicious can sometimes pour affliction upon the good, their power is transient and their punishment certain; and that innocence, though oppressed by injustice, shall, supported by patience, finally triumph over misfortune!'[7] Matilda, in Eliza Parsons's *Castle of Wolfenbach,* restored to her rights as the daughter of the Countess Berniti, enunciates the moral in a letter she writes to Mother St Magdalene: ' "From you," said she, "I learned resignation, and a dependence on that Being who never forsakes the virtuous; from you I learned never to despair . . . I shall ever remember the unfortunate have claims upon the hearts of those whom God has blessed with affluence; and that, through your means, reserved to experience every blessing of life, I shall feel it my duty, by active virtues, to extend, to the utmost of my abilities, those blessings to others less fortunate than myself." '[8]

The strident tones and crude attempts at emphasis, often through typographical devices of capitalization, italics, and

designed to test the reader's own evaluation of character—a truly perspicacious judge will share Radcliffe's premise that virtuous characters do not change and will not entertain a doubt about their innocence. On the other hand, it seems an odd violation of trust between an author and a character she admires that some of the most interesting suspense of the novel should be generated by a position that Radcliffe ethically cannot support.

[5] Ann Radcliffe, *A Sicilian Romance,* new edn. (2 vols., London, 1821; repr. 2 vols. in 1, New York, 1972), ii. 216.

[6] Clara Reeve, *The Old English Baron: A Gothic Story,* ed. J. Trainer (London, 1967), p. 153.

[7] Ann Radcliffe, *The Mysteries of Udolpho: A Romance,* ed. B. Dobrée (London, 1970), p. 672.

[8] Eliza Parsons, *Castle of Wolfenbach* (London, 1793; repr. London, 1968), p. 179.

spacing, reveal a mingled determination to be explicit about the moral lessons to be gained from such tales of adventure and an uncertainty about the relevance of those 'lessons' to the narrative that has produced them. Mary-Anne Radcliffe thus concludes *Manfroné; or, The One-Handed Monk* by arguing that her unrelieved tale of the vices of mankind has been designed to show the beauty and superiority of goodness:

Here the pen pauses: with its weak efforts it has endeavoured to delineate the vices of mankind, placing them in such a glaring view, with the hope of exciting in the bosom of the reader that horror and detestation which must make him studiously avoid giving way to those turbulent passions that vitiate the mind, and render it insensible to the charms of virtue; and may these pages, which shew him the misery attendant on evil actions, in all his researches after worldly enjoyment and felicity, deeply impress on his mind, beyond the prevailing power of vice to erase, the never-failing maxim, that

'To be good is to be happy!'[9]

MORALIZING

In such Gothic novels as Sophia Lee's *The Recess* and Ann Radcliffe's *The Castles of Athlin and Dunbayne,* the tendency of the narrative voice to make confident generalizations about human behaviour has a similar stabilizing effect, because it suggests, as, for example, in Fielding's *Tom Jones,* that the reader is in the hands of a thoughtful and wise director, whose moral values resemble his own.[10] Charlotte Dacre's *Zofloya* opens with a description of the main characters, doomed early in life because of their mother's transgression with an unprincipled count. Throughout the setting of this scene, Dacre intrudes to moralize on child-rearing, self-love, and depravity. On the Marchese's attempt to correct the defects of Victoria's nature—defects that will later involve her in several murders and cause her to sell her soul to the devil—she writes:

Vainly did the Marchese hope that time, by maturing her reason, and improving her ideas, would correct the wrong bias of her

[9] Mary-Anne Radcliffe, *Manfroné; or, The One-Handed Monk. A Romance,* 3rd edn. (4 vols., London, 1828; repr. 4 vols. in 2, New York, 1972), iv. 221–2.

[10] On the effects of this moral stance on the novels of Ann Radcliffe, see P. Lewis, 'Fearful Lessons: The Didacticism of the Early Gothic Novel', *College Language Association Journal,* xxiii (1980), 470–84.

character; for strict education alone can correct the faults in our nature; they will not correct themselves. If improper tendencies are engendered by early neglect, education may still work a reform; for we are in a great measure the creatures of education, rather than of organisation: the former can almost always surmount the defects of the latter. Thus, though Victoria in childhood gave proofs of what is termed, somewhat injudiciously, a corrupt nature, yet a firm and decided course of education would so far have changed her bent, that those propensities, which by neglect became vices, might have been ameliorated into virtues.[11]

In *Castle of Wolfenbach* there is a similar tendency to merge the dramatic with the authorial or editorial, so that what often begins as a conversation ends as a moral message delivered directly to the reader from the author. In one such passage, Matilda is explaining to the Countess of Wolfenbach the advances made towards her by her supposed uncle:

'It was plain my uncle had taken notice of my coldness, and complained to her: I was mortified and vexed; after taking two or three turns I went into the house, and met my uncle in the breakfast room; I assumed the kindest manner possible in my salutations to him, and I saw he was highly gratified by it. He produced his books and drawings, the latter were very beautiful, but the attitudes and want of decent drapery confused and hurt me, for although I had never received any particular lessons on delicacy or modesty, yet there is that innate virtuous principle within us, that shrinks involuntarily from any thing tending to violate that sense of decency we are all, I believe, born with . . .'[12]

Even in situations in which the moral has been pointed dramatically, it is not uncommon for Gothic writers to underline it rhetorically, as if they are doubtful of the impact of a simply dramatic lesson. Thus, the dying Count of Wolfenbach rather sophistically draws Eliza Parsons's moral from his life of vice:

'I now thank heaven that both you and Joseph are alive, and adore the ways of Providence, who extracts good out of evil, and made the very crimes I intended to perpetrate the means of deliverance to you both. The death of the unfortunate Chevalier I bitterly repent, and

[11] Charlotte Dacre, *Zofloya; or, The Moor: A Romance of the Fifteenth Century* (3 vols., London, 1806; repr. New York, 1974), i. 34–5. A romance beloved by Shelley, *Zofloya* exercised an influence on his *Zastrozzi* (1810) and *St. Irvyne* (1811).

[12] *Castle of Wolfenbach*, p. 12.

can only observe here, that when a man gives himself up to unrestrained passions of what nature soever, one vicious indulgence leads to another, crimes succeed each other, and to veil one, and avoid discoveries, we are drawn insensibly to the commission of such detestable actions as once we most abhorred the idea of: for, although my temper was not good, and my passions always violent, had not love and jealousy urged me to desperation, and deprived me of reason, my soul would have shrunk at the thoughts of murders, which grew at last necessary for my preservation.'[13]

The tendency of Gothic characters to speak in highly generalized, non-particularized terms is remarkable, for it emphasizes not only the relative flatness of their characters, but the inclination in Gothic works of the moral to intrude on—and often overshadow—the dramatic. In *Castle of Wolfenbach*, interestingly, most of the violent, Gothic elements of the novel are not presented by means of enacted situations at all, but through interpolated stories of injustice told by victims and perpetrators. The violence of the tale, with the exception of the bloody moment in which Matilda finds the servant of the Countess of Wolfenbach, is thus filtered for the reader because it is presented at a second remove from the actual event.

Radcliffe's novels also display this predilection: 'It is the peculiar attribute of great minds,' the author interrupts in *The Castles of Athlin and Dunbayne*, 'to bear up with increasing force against the shock of misfortune; with them the nerves of resistance strengthen with attack; and they may be said to subdue adversity with her own weapons.'[14] In Radcliffe's later novels, authorial commentary becomes less frequent; the moralizing urge still exists, but its burden is increasingly shifted to her characters, who frequently utter generalizations about human nature in dialogues or sometimes wearying apostrophes. 'The world', muses St Aubert, in an example of such a passage, 'ridicules a passion which it seldom feels; its scenes, and its interests, distract the mind, deprave the taste, corrupt the heart, and love cannot exist in a heart that has lost the meek dignity of innocence. Virtue and taste are nearly the same, for virtue is little more than active taste, and the most

[13] Ibid., 137.

[14] Ann Radcliffe, *The Castles of Athlin and Dunbayne. A Highland Story*, new edn. (London, 1821; repr. New York, 1972), p. 35.

delicate affections of each combine in real love. How then are we to look for love in great cities, where selfishness, dissipation, and insincerity supply the place of tenderness, simplicity and truth?'[15] The slowing of pace and abstract quality of the diction here point to the difficulty of fitting the generalizing authorial voice to a character engaged in a dramatic situation. Such reflective interludes are frequent in Radcliffe's work and contribute to that quality of meditativeness that characterizes her novels; the intention, ultimately, seems to be to assure the reader that, even in the midst of events that defy his usual sense of what is possible, normal ethical codes are still in operation. The tacit assurance is that what appears on the surface to be a fantastic or unjust series of incidents will eventually be resolved, and in a fashion consistent with what is morally right.

What is sometimes perplexing about this moralizing tendency, however, is that in the lesser novels of the genre it often assumes a disjunctive relationship to the action that supposedly inspires it. Thus, in Mary-Anne Radcliffe's *Manfroné*, a rhapsodic speech on the transitory and delusive nature of human joys accords but ill with the adventures of dark forms and folded mantles that will shortly interrupt it. The disruptive combination of the two modes of narrating is seen in the description of Montalto's wounding: 'The soul of Montalto, calm and full of content, communicated its repose to its mortal habitation, and the happy lover, slumbering, became unconscious of what was passing around him— —became unconscious of a dark savage form that hung over him, and who, putting his hand within the folds of his mantle, drew from thence a dagger!—Ah! where was then the guardian spirit which watches over the safety of the virtuous?'[16] The hackneyed, metaphoric use of images of gulfs, brinks, and graves in such moralizing passages inadvertently calls to our attention how uncomfortably such idioms sit with narratives that revolve so insistently around the real thing:

How transitory, how delusive are human joys! when we think we hold the phantom happiness in our grasp, it vanishes! Always in pursuit, yet we never attain it . . . Still, however, we fondly look forward, and in fancy see the air-formed gorgeous temple of human happiness rising

[15] *The Mysteries of Udolpho*, pp. 49–50. [16] *Manfroné*, iv. 31.

stately before us—we see its wide-folding portals open to receive us—when, alas! we suddenly awake, and find it was but a mere delusion of the brain—a delusion which made us mindless of the wide-yawning gulf, on whose dreadful brink we totter, and often are lost.[17]

The lack of self-consciousness in a passage such as this one is startling; the author shifts from one rhetorical mode to the next with no apparent awareness of disjunction or collision.

This tendency of a sermonizing tone to deepen the reader's sense of disruption is occasionally manifested on the level of the novel's plot. Sometimes, in fact, an author's moralizing serves as a mask beneath which he may adjust events to fit the forthcoming needs of the story. Thus, again in *Manfroné*, when Father Augustino dies, the narrator exclaims, 'What a pleasing, soul-elevating sight it is to behold the last sighs of the just!'[18] The point of the scene, however, is not to moralize about death, but to remove Father Augustino from the story so that the Marchese di Montalto can appear at the attempted marriage of Rosalina and Manfroné.

In the novels of Lewis, Shelley, or Maturin, the difficulties of contending with such moral commentary increase. In Shelley's *Zastrozzi,* it is ominously absent; in *The Monk* and *Melmoth the Wanderer,* narrative interpolations have an effect of disturbing rather than orienting the reader:

Scarcely had the Abbey-Bell tolled for five minutes [Lewis begins *The Monk*], and already was the Church of the Capuchins thronged with Auditors. Do not encourage the idea that the Crowd was assembled either from motives of piety or thirst of information. But very few were influenced by those reasons; and in a city where superstition reigns with such despotic sway as in Madrid, to seek for true devotion would be a fruitless attempt.[19]

The opening of Melmoth's tale is similarly destructive to a full sense of participation on the part of the reader; it is interlarded with a puzzlingly irrelevant and unconnected profusion of literary allusions: 'No one knew so well as she', Maturin writes in a particularly garbled passage, 'to find where the four streams met, in which, on the same portentous season, the chemise was to be immersed, and then displayed before the

[17] Ibid., iv. 26–7.
[18] Ibid., i. 201.
[19] Matthew Lewis, *The Monk: A Romance,* ed. H. Anderson (London, 1973), p. 7.

fire, (in the name of one whom we dare not mention to "ears polite"), to be turned by the figure of the destined husband before morning.'[20] Maturin's repeated intrusions of learned material into his supernatural narrative violate the tone in odd ways: John Melmoth is said to pore over the crumbling manuscript of Stanton's temptation like an antiquarian hoping to find 'some unutterable abomination of Petronius or Martial, happily elucidatory of the mysteries of the Spintriæ, or the orgies of the Phallic worshippers'.[21] By the time Monçada's tale is introduced, Maturin's work has developed a sinister and unrelieved congruity of tone; the incongruities that precede it, however, are so extreme as to appear almost burlesque.

GOTHIC HISTORICIZING

Earlier 'historical Gothic' novels are not so encumbered by the need for a helpful narrating voice: validated by their supposed fidelity to recorded history, they usually emphasize their special authority in their prefaces or introductory paragraphs. Thomas Leland's *Longsword*, for example, a novel based on the life of William Longsword, third Earl of Salisbury, acknowledges at the outset its debt to ancient English histories. Similarly, Sophia Lee, in her historical romance, *The Recess,* draws, as does Walpole, upon an 'obsolete' and fragmented manuscript, claiming that 'an inviolable respect for truth' has prevented her from connecting the events omitted by the original narrative.[22] Once such novels are anchored in the historical past, the events themselves are inevitably adjusted to fit the novelists' purposes, and anachronisms and improbabilities abound. This cavalier attitude towards past times was often a target of abuse for early critics of 'historical Gothic'. Though Lee's sister, Harriet (with whom Sophia would later collaborate in *The Canterbury Tales* (1797–1805)), declared that *The Recess* was 'the first English romance that blended interesting fiction with historical events

[20] Charles Robert Maturin, *Melmoth the Wanderer: A Tale,* ed. D. Grant (London, 1968), p. 11.

[21] Ibid., 58.

[22] Sophia Lee, *The Recess; or, A Tale of Other Times* (3 vols., London, 1783–5; repr. New York, 1972), i. viii.

and characters, embellishing both by picturesque description',[23] others, including Richard Graves, were less charmed by her distortions of history. A maiden lady in the postscript to his *Plexippus,* who has read *The Recess,* declares that Mary Stuart cannot be defended because she had two bastards by the Duke of Norfolk.[24]

Ann Radcliffe was frequently taken to task for 'mutilating' history and customs in this way.[25] Her anachronistic references to Salvator Rosa in *The Mysteries of Udolpho* and to the poetry of Gray in *The Castles of Athlin and Dunbayne* suggest that she is not so much concerned with a verifiable historical period as with an atmosphere recently made familiar to an eighteenth-century audience through the artists of the picturesque. 'There is some fancy and much romantic imagery in the conduct of this story', wrote a reviewer of *The Castles of Athlin and Dunbayne;* 'but our pleasure would have been more unmixed had our author preserved better the manners and costume of the Highlands. He seems to be unacquainted with both.'[26] In a satirical letter on 'Terrorist Novel Writing' in *The Spirit of the Public Journals,* Radcliffe comes under even more severe attack:

> The *system of terror* which [Ann Radcliffe] has adopted is not the only reproach to which she is liable. Besides the tedious monotony of her descriptions, she affects in the most disgusting manner a knowledge of languages, countries, customs, and objects of art, of which she is lamentably ignorant. She suspends *tripods* from the ceiling by chains, not knowing that a *tripod* is a utensil standing upon three feet. She covers the kingdom of Naples with India figs, because *St Pierre* has introduced those tropical plants in his tales, of which the scene is laid in India, and she makes a convent of monks a necessary appendage to a monastery of nuns. . . . Whenever she introduces an Italian word, it is sure to be a gross violation of the language. Instead of making a nobleman's servant call him *Padrone,* or

[23] Harriet Lee, Preface to *The Canterbury Tales,* rev. and corr. (2 vols., London, 1832; repr. New York, 1978), i. vi.

[24] *Plexippus: or, The Aspiring Plebeian* (2 vols., London, 1790), i. xi–xii.

[25] The verb recurs in the critical literature with some frequency: '[Our author]', writes the reviewer of *The Castle of Mowbray. An English Romance,* 'has mutilated history, is unacquainted with the human heart, and deficient in judgment; yet with these defects, he enters the lists as the rival of Horace Walpole, and Miss Lee' (*Critical Review,* lxvi (1788), 577).

[26] *Critical Review,* lxviii (1789), 251.

Illustrissimo, she makes him address him by the title of *Maestro,* which is Italian for a teacher; she converts the singular of *Lazzaroni* into *Lazzaro,* &c. &c. &c.[27]

Radcliffe's are the venial errors of a writer eager to produce an effect and not concerned to verify certain of the more exotic details of her settings or language. In the lesser works of the genre, this lack of sensitivity to setting and costume may be so pervasive that the characters appear (somewhat awkwardly) to be enacting the rituals of an eighteenth-century English drawing room in some incongruous place and time. As Scott complained of the imitators of Walpole's *Castle of Otranto*, '. . . amid all their attempts to assume the tone of antique chivalry, something occurs in every chapter so decidedly incongruous, as at once reminds us of an ill-sustained masquerade, in which ghosts, knights-errant, magicians, and damsels gent, are all equipped in hired dresses from the same warehouse in Tavistock-street.'[28]

Not all reviewers of Gothic fiction objected this strenuously to the 'historical veneering' of tales of romance. Such embellishments, indeed, seemed to some to 'sober down' the stories, to tame and justify some of their more extravagant flights into the supernatural. The remarks of the *Critical Review* for 1762 on Leland's *Longsword* reflect this stand:

> We are indebted to the author of this work for the introduction of a new and agreeable species of writing, in which the beauties of poetry, and the advantages of history are happily united. The story of this *romance* . . . is founded on real facts, and without doing any great violence to truth, pleases the imagination, at the same time that it improves the heart.[29]

Leland, in truth, creates less tonal disharmony in merging history and romance than, for example, Walpole, who goes to great pains in the 'Translator's Preface' of *The Castle of Otranto* to locate the narrative 'between 1095, the æra of the first crusade, and 1243, the date of the last, or not long after-

[27] 'Terrorist Novel Writing', *Spirit of the Public Journals,* i (1797), 227.

[28] [Sir Walter Scott], in his introd. to *The Castle of Otranto; A Gothic Story* (Edinburgh, 1811), p. xxii.

[29] Review of Thomas Leland, *Longsword Earl of Salisbury: An Historical Romance,* in the *Critical Review,* xiii (1762), 252.

wards',[30] and then violates that precision in the chaotic tale that follows. Authenticity here, as in many Gothic works, becomes merely an excuse for licence—as does the tendency to set the tales in 'other places' or at 'other times'.

PROVIDENTIAL, SENTIMENTAL, AND DECORATIVE GOTHIC

Gothic novels may be generically stabilized by hearkening back to the procedures and language not only of history but of older, recognized fictional modes. Radcliffe's novels in particular, and the late 'sentimental Gothic' fiction of Roche and Parsons, exhibit a regard for providential meetings and rescues that recalls the works of Fielding or Goldsmith. Adeline, in *The Romance of the Forest,* persecuted by La Motte and the Marquis, is thus said at the end to survive by 'a destiny . . . to punish the murderer of her parent. When a retrospect is taken of the vicissitudes and dangers to which she had been exposed from her earliest infancy, it appears as if her preservation was the effect of something more than human policy, and affords a striking instance that Justice, however long delayed, will overtake the guilty.'[31] Julia, in *A Sicilian Romance*, is similarly convinced that providence has 'conducted [her] through a labyrinth of misfortunes to this spot, for the purpose of delivering [her mother]'.[32] The emphasis is even more overt in the earlier works of Leland and Reeve. 'I adored', proclaims Longsword, 'the preserving hand of heaven, whose influence had appeared so evidently in these events. The treachery of D'Aumont in seeking to destroy me, had opportunely conveyed me from the power of my enemies. The violence and oppression of Chauvigny, had proved the means of sending me deliverers, when fortune seemed most to frown upon me . . . '[33] The passage sounds almost like Defoe: Longsword assumes the

[30] Horace Walpole, *The Castle of Otranto: A Gothic Story,* ed. W. S. Lewis (London, 1969), p. 3.

[31] *The Romance of the Forest,* iii. 257.

[32] *A Sicilian Romance,* ii. 175–6.

[33] Thomas Leland, *Longsword, Earl of Salisbury: An Historical Romance,* ed. J. C. Stephens, jun. (New York, 1957), p. 47.

familiar retrospective stance that clarifies events that have been shrouded in mystery and speaks in syntactically balanced clauses that demonstrate the relationship between apparent evil and universal good.

Coincidences abound in Gothic fiction and are regularly attributed to the effects of providential supervision; heroes inevitably appear in the nick of time, at the most unlikely times, and in the most unlikely places. The reader is not meant to be surprised, but tantalized, when Manfroné discovers his own hand washed up on the shores of Lake Abruzzo. Even ghosts—the question of whose existence is often a source of embarrassment to Gothic writers—are tentatively put down to the infinite power of providence. As Madame de Menon muses to Emilia and Julia in an interesting passage in *A Sicilian Romance,*

> 'Who shall say that any thing is impossible to God? We know that he has made us, who are embodied spirits; he, therefore, can make unembodied spirits. If we cannot understand how such spirits exist, we should consider the limited powers of our minds, and that we cannot understand many things which are indisputably true. . . . Such spirits, if indeed they have ever been seen, can have appeared only by the express permission of God, and for some very singular purposes; be assured that there are no beings who act unseen by him; and that, therefore, there are none from whom innocence can ever suffer harm.'[34]

These are curious observations, because Radcliffe finally in her novels regularly attributes all ghost-like effects to human agency; here, she seems to amuse herself with the thought that ghosts exist, but then evades the larger consequences of this view by attributing the possibility in the most conventional way to the hand of God.[35] In *The Old English Baron,* Reeve's insistence on the effects of providential agency often creates—in a similar way to the works of Defoe and Smollett—interesting tensions between the stasis or stability achieved by the providential view and the forward impetus required by the narrative of adven-

[34] *A Sicilian Romance,* i. 83–4.

[35] Such attributions are a regular feature of eighteenth-century supernatural tales. In one sense, enjoyment of the Gothic depends precisely on this flirtatious willingness to accept temporarily a dictum not commonly or generally held.

ture: 'Doubt not, said Oswald, but Heaven, who has evidently conducted you by the hand thus far, will compleat its own work; for my part, I can only wonder and adore!—Give me your advice then, said Edmund; for Heaven assists us by natural means'.[36] The final sentence of *The Old English Baron* strikes an unmistakably Christian note: 'All these [papers], when together, furnish a striking lesson to posterity, of the over-ruling hand of Providence, and the certainty of RETRIBUTION.'[37] Thus one must be, perhaps, more cautious about generalizing, as do Nelson and Hume, about the degree to which the Gothic is a form marked by the disappearance of God.[38] Early Gothic works emphatically exhibit the same complex plots and the same attentiveness to providential coincidence as did their forebears and often adopt the same language to talk about it. Indeed, many of the first Gothic romances are simply moral tales in supernatural dress—the Gothic elements, that is, do not transform the structure of the narrative in any significant way; rather, they readorn and refurbish what to its readers would have been an old familiar form. This is certainly James R. Foster's view of the Gothic; to him, the mode is not revolutionary at all, but takes its place within a tradition of sentimental novel writing influenced primarily by Prévost:

> The true nature of the so-called Gothic novel has been misunderstood . . . The critics who have hit upon supernaturalism as the most distinctive and significant element, have done this in spite of the fact that a part of the body of the fiction they pretend to describe is plainly controlled by a rationalism that forbids anything more than a mere toying with the appearances of the marvellous . . .
>
> The novel which reached a phase of its development with Ann Radcliffe played with ghosts, but its main purpose was obviously to tell a sentimental tale of adventure. . . .[39]

[36] *The Old English Baron,* p. 63.

[37] Ibid., 153.

[38] L. Nelson, jun., 'Night Thoughts on the Gothic Novel', *Yale Review,* lii (1962), 251; R. D. Hume, 'Gothic Versus Romantic: A Revaluation of the Gothic Novel', *PMLA* lxxxiv (1969), 287; 289.

[39] J. R. Foster, 'The Abbé Prevost and the English Novel', *PMLA* xlii (1927), 443. Foster elaborates on this view in his *History of the Pre-romantic Novel in England,*

Contemporary critics often responded to this connection by speaking of Gothic fiction in terms reserved for the novel of sentiment. Thus, the author of the letter, 'Terrorist Novel Writing', exposes Gothic romance by testing it against the sentimental and moral criteria it seems to invite:

> . . . confining the heroes and heroines in old gloomy castles . . . is now so common, that a novelist blushes to bring about a marriage by ordinary means, but conducts the happy pair through long and dangerous galleries, where the light burns blue . . . Are the duties of life so changed, that all the instruction necessary for a young person is to learn to walk at night upon the battlements of an old castle, to creep hands and feet along a narrow passage, and meet the devil at the end of it? . . . Can our young ladies be taught nothing more necessary in life, than to sleep in a dungeon with venemous reptiles, walk through a ward with assassins, and carry bloody daggers in their pockets, instead of pin-cushions and needle-books?[40]

It is difficult to dismiss such a critique as reactionary or conservative, for many Gothic novelists spoke openly about the sentimental nature of their endeavours. Many, like Clara Reeve, Regina Maria Roche, and Eliza Parsons, showed themselves adept at both genres, and many sentimental novelists (among them Charlotte Smith) in turn made free use of Gothic devices. The link, indeed, between Gothic and sentimental fiction is strong: both modes assume the primacy of feeling, and the pleasure of exercising it vicariously, and gain their effect by encouraging particularly strong emotional responses from their readers. The forms can overlap because it is the intensity of the response and not the type of experience eliciting the response (pleasurable, terrifying) that is in question. Gothic novels are,

Modern Language Association Monograph Series, xvii (New York, 1949), 186–7: 'The Gothic romance, especially as written by eighteenth-century ladies, is a sentimental novel in which the characters are tricked out in costumes belonging to some past epoch but rarely concealing the fact that the minds and manners of the wearers really belong to the century of enlightenment. . . . Gothicism was a new plaything for the sentimental imagination'. Foster's use of metaphors of clothing and costuming emphasizes his conviction that the Gothic is essentially a mode of appliqué wrought on a conventional fictional form.

[40] 'Terrorist Novel Writing', 227–9.

thus, replete with sentimental episodes: love affairs between young unfortunates generally occupy the centre of the plot and scenes of fainting and melancholy yearning are frequent. The plight of Parsons's Matilda in *Castle of Wolfenbach* is, in fact, more Richardsonian than Gothic. Pursued by the B-like Mr Weimar, Matilda has just overheard her uncle and his confidante, the Jewkes-like Agatha, plotting her ruin in the summer-house. Her response (like that of many of Parsons's and Roche's leading ladies) is directly in the sentimental tradition: 'Having heard thus far I tottered from the summer-house, and got into the shrubbery, where I threw myself on the ground, and preserved myself from fainting by a copious flood of tears!'[41] Matilda escapes with her servant that night. Clara Reeve claimed in her dedication to *The Exiles* that 'it has always been my aim to support the cause of morality, to reprove vice, and to promote all the social and domestic virtues',[42] and her *Old English Baron* originally bore a more adamant (if less romantic) title: *The Champion of Virtue*. Regina Maria Roche's highly popular *The Children of the Abbey*, a novel almost as beloved as Radcliffe's *Mysteries of Udolpho* in its time, and often described as Gothic in tone, is thoroughly sentimental in nature with only one incident—that of Amanda's discovery of Lady Dunreath in the castle—that could be called truly Gothic. A set of instructions for transforming a Gothic romance into a sentimental novel in the anonymous poem, *The Age*, reveals a humorous awareness of the fundamental similarities between the two forms:

> The conduct of the poet in considering romances and novels separately, may be thought singular by those who have penetration to see that a novel may be made out of a romance, or a romance out of a novel with the greatest ease, by scratching out a few terms, and inserting others. Take the following, which may, like machinery in factories, accelerate the progress of the divine art.

[41] *Castle of Wolfenbach*, p. 13.

[42] Clara Reeve, *The Exiles; or, Memoirs of the Count de Cronstadt* (3 vols., London, 1788), i. xiii.

From any romance to make a novel.
Where you find—

A castle,	put An house.
A cavern,	A bower.
A groan,	A sigh.
A giant,	A father.
A blood-stained dagger,	A fan.
Howling blasts,	Zephyrs.
A knight,	A gentleman without whiskers.
A lady who is the heroine,	Need not be changed, being versatile.
Assassins,	Killing glances.
A monk,	An old steward.
Skeletons, skulls, &c.,	Compliments, sentiments, &c.
A lamp,	A candle.
A magic book sprinkled with blood,	A letter bedewed with tears.
Mysterious voices,	Abstruse words, (easily found in a dictionary).
A secret oath,	A tender hint accompanied with naiveté.
A gliding ghost,	A usurer, or an attorney.
A witch,	An old housekeeper.
A wound,	A kiss.
A midnight murder,	A marriage.

The same table of course answers for transmuting a novel into a romance.[43]

This essentially decorative effect of the Gothic has repeatedly been condemned by critics and has made the form particularly vulnerable to satire. Most of the novels gain resonance and continuity by making use of the same devices: ruined castles, secret panels, concealed portraits, underground passageways. There is surprisingly little variation on this design. Even in more sophisticated examples of the genre, such as the novels of Maturin, where the devices, bolstered by other aspects of the

[43] *The Age; A Poem: Moral, Political, and Metaphysical. With Illustrative Annotations. In Ten Books* (London, 1810), pp. 209–10 n. 1.

narrative, become more psychologically suggestive, they occupy an undeniably prominent position. In extreme cases—those of Reeve or Lee, for example—the essential 'Gothicness' of the work attaches almost exclusively to these properties. An attempt to isolate the distinctive qualities of Gothic narrative brings the reader repeatedly back to this characteristic: Gothicism is finally much less about evil, 'the fascination of the abomination',[44] than it is a standardized, absolutely formulaic system of creating a certain kind of atmosphere in which a reader's sensibility toward fear and horror is exercised in predictable ways. To include 'modern Gothic' novels such as *Wuthering Heights, Moby Dick,* and *Sanctuary* in the same category as Radcliffe's *The Italian* or Lewis's *The Monk* because they have in common 'a distinctive and pervasive atmosphere [of evil]'[45] is to overlook the primacy of such a system. This is not a popular stand to take towards the Gothic because much of the more spirited recent criticism of the genre has been explicitly directed towards denying that it is 'a collection of ghost-story devices'.[46] Underlying such reassessments is the assumption that psychological or moral ambiguity—of the kind present in *Wuthering Heights, Moby Dick,* and *Sanctuary,* but not in Ann Radcliffe's works—lends a dignity to the form that the emphasis on Gothic properties threatens to jeopardize. The devices, thus, in a critical sleight of hand that here seems particularly out of place, become necessarily signifiers of some deeper meaning. Any honest reading of Gothic fiction shows that the pleasure—and not the despair—of the text arises fairly forthrightly from the repetition of a certain series of extremely conventional scenes, events, and landscapes. The superficial and the formulaic thus, paradoxically, form the very heart of the Gothic, and because of this, the genre can acquire stability across itself (as television serials do) by making repeated use of the same interesting settings and events. Keats's letter to Reynolds of 1818 exhibits the kind of delight that an exaggerated attention to the formulaic

[44] Robert L. Platzner urges this view. See Platzner and R. D. Hume, ' "Gothic Versus Romantic": A Rejoinder', *PMLA* lxxxvi (1971), 266–7.

[45] Hume, 'Gothic Versus Romantic', 287. The broadness of a classificatory system that associates Gothic and evil is in part responsible for the lingering of the term 'Gothic' to describe, for example, the stories of Poe.

[46] Ibid., 282.

can produce: '. . . I am going among Scenery whence I intend to tip you the Damosel Radcliffe', he writes, '—I'll cavern you, and grotto you, and waterfall you, and wood you, and immense-rock you, and tremendous sound you, and solitude you.'[47] Scott's response, and that of many contemporary reviewers of the Gothic who repeatedly offered 'recipes' for modern romance, is more disgruntled:

We strolled [Scott writes in a discussion of current Gothic fiction in the *Quarterly Review*] through a variety of castles, each of which was regularly called Il Castello; met with as many captains of condottieri; heard various ejaculations of Santa Maria and Diabolo; read by a decaying lamp, and in a tapestried chamber, dozens of legends as stupid as the main history; examined such suites of deserted apartments as might fit up a reasonable barrack; and saw as many glimmering lights as would make a respectable illumination. . . .[48]

The recipes of 'Anti Ghost' and of the author of 'Terrorist Novel Writing' proceed along similar lines:

Take an old castle [directs 'Anti Ghost']; pull down a part of it, and allow the grass to grow on the battlements, and provide the owls and bats with uninterrupted habitations among the ruins. Pour a sufficient quantity of heavy rain upon the hinges and bolts of the gates, so that when they are attempted to be opened, they may creak most fearfully. Next take an old man and woman, and employ them to sleep in a part of this castle, and provide them with frightful stories of lights that appear in the western or the eastern tower every night, and of music heard in the neighbouring woods, and ghosts dressed in white who perambulate the place.

Convey to this castle a young lady: consign her to the care of the old man and woman, who must relate to her all they know, that is all they do not know, but only suspect. Make her dreadfully terrified at the relation, but dreadfully impatient to behold the reality. Convey her, perhaps on the second night of her arrival, through a trap-door, and from the trap-door to a flight of steps downwards, and from a flight of steps to a subterraneous passage, and from a subterraneous passage, to a door that is shut, and from that to a door that is open, and from that to a cell, and from that to a chapel, and from a chapel back to a subterraneous passage again; here present either a skeleton with a live face, or a living body with the head of a skeleton, or a

[47] Keats to J. H. Reynolds, 14 Mar. 1818, no. 68, in *The Letters of John Keats 1814–1821*, ed. H. E. Rollins (2 vols., Cambridge, Mass., 1958), i. 245.

[48] Review of *Fatal Revenge*, in the *Quarterly Review*, iii (1810), 341.

ghost all in white, or a groan from a distant part of a cavern, or the shake of a cold hand, or a suit of armour moving—fierce 'put out the light, and then'—

Let this be repeated for some nights in succession, and after the lady has been dissolved to a jelly with her fears, let her be delivered by the man of her heart, and married—*Probatum est.*[49]

It was, of course, this predilection for the formula—and the ease with which it was copied—that allowed the proliferation and final degeneration of the form into the 'shilling shockers' or 'bluebooks' of the early nineteenth century.[50]

PROBLEMS OF CHARACTER

The Gothic novelists' interest in the device may not at first appear to pose any particular problems—novels of this kind, the argument runs, exempt themselves from serious consideration because of their obvious superficiality. But the adherence to formulas (basically a technique of the surface) signals a concern with the superficial that, as Eve Sedgwick and Coral Ann Howells have pointed out, finds its way into other, more significant facets of the genre's form, and particularly into character. Sedgwick's exploration of this attribute of the Gothic illuminates the important repercussions of such a technique:

. . . the fascination with the code in Gothic novels is so full and imperious that it weakens the verbal supports for the fiction of presence . . .

It is in the insistence of this constitutive struggle, and the attenuated versions involving the veil and the habit rather than the countenance itself, that the Gothic novel makes its most radical contribution to the development of character in fiction. In a (novelistic) world of faces where the diacritical code is poor but where all nonlinguistic, or nonsignifying, discriminations are elided in its favor . . . two things will happen. First, there will be unbounded confusions of identity along the few diacritical axes: any furrowed man will be

[49] 'On the New Method of Inculcating Morality' [Letter to the editor], in *Walker's Hibernian Magazine; or, Compendium of Entertaining Knowledge* (1798), pt. i, p. 12.

[50] On the shilling shockers, see W. W. Watt, *Shilling Shockers of the Gothic School: A Study of Chapbook Gothic Romances,* Harvard Honors Theses in English, v (Cambridge, Mass., 1932; repr. New York, 1967). On Lane's involvement in the popularization of Gothic romance, see D. Blakey, *The Minerva Press 1790–1820* (Printed for the Bibliographical Society at the University Press, Oxford, 1939 (for 1935)).

confusable with any other furrowed man (Schedoni with Zampari with Zeluca, for example), and so forth. Second, when the time comes to settle these confusions, the normal tools for doing so—nonce discriminations, the differentiations that happen not to be coded, 'This one has blue eyes and that one, I remember, had brown eyes . . .' —will be unavailable. The noncode level of discriminations having been vitiated by the fascination of the code, the only reliable basis for comparison will be one of those complete literal, ocular juxtapositions. And that will be reliable only to the degree that the two faces approach being line-for-line identical. (I.e., there is such a thing as a decided 'Yes! They are exactly the same' but no possible criterion for a decided 'No.') There seem to be no noncoded differences between persons that could not also occur in any one person over time.[51]

The almost exclusive concern with two-dimensional characters in the Gothic becomes obvious when one attempts to discriminate between characters of different works: Radcliffe's heroines, Julia, Adeline, Emily, and Ellena, as was frequently observed by critics in Radcliffe's time, are a case in point:

Her heroines too nearly resemble each other, or rather they possess hardly any shade of difference. They have all blue eyes and auburn hair—the form of each of them has 'the airy lightness of a nymph' —they are all fond of watching the setting sun, and catching the purple tints of evening, and the vivid glow or fading splendour of the western horizon. Unfortunately they are all likewise early risers. I say unfortunately, for in every exigency Mrs. Radcliffe's heroines are provided with a pencil and paper, and the sun is never allowed to rise or set in peace. Like Tilburina in the play, they are 'inconsolable to the minuet in Ariadne,' and in the most distressing circumstances find time to compose sonnets to sun-rise, the bat, a sea-nymph, a lily, or a butterfly.[52]

Even conversation, muffled by the dictates of convention, provides no key to their inner minds: ' . . . particulars of individual feeling are blurred by orthodox rhetoric, and conversation is restricted by decorum to being a statement of the outward appearance of emotion'.[53] What we are finally given, in Howells's

[51] E. K. Sedgwick, 'The Character in the Veil: Imagery of the Surface in the Gothic Novel', *PMLA* xcvi (1981), 263.

[52] J. C. Dunlop, *History of Prose Fiction,* rev. edn. (2 vols., London, 1888), ed. H. Wilson, ii. 581.

[53] C. A. Howells, *Love, Mystery, and Misery: Feeling in Gothic Fiction* (London, 1978), p. 24.

words, are 'gestures of feeling', 'external details of emotional display' rather than 'any insight into the complexity of the feelings themselves'.[54] This emphasis on the superficial not only marks Gothic characters' personalities and actions; it is often used as a device to generate suspense about those characters. The supposed orphan Matilda in *Castle of Wolfenbach* (who at the end of the novel turns out to be the daughter of the Countess Berniti) is repeatedly referred to as gentle in countenance and bearing. '[H]er person, her figure, the extraordinary natural understanding she possesses', the Marquis exclaims, 'confirms my opinion that so many graces seldom belong to a mean birth or dishonest connexions'.[55] The servant Bertha detects her goodness immediately, and the Countess of Wolfenbach, whose chambers are accidentally visited by Matilda, tells her that her countenance 'is a letter of recommendation to every heart'.[56] The reader's recognition of Matilda's gentility, in a novel that places little emphasis on the exploration of internal states, must be accomplished through outward signs. Howells thus speaks convincingly of the 'theatricality' of the Gothic, of its emphasis on dramatic action and visual display. Walpole's characters, denied the language of the heart, act out the passions that move them in highly physical ways: Frederic, consumed with guilt at his passion for Matilda, falls to the ground 'in a conflict of penitence and passion'.[57] A confusingly disproportionate relationship develops here that deserves examination: the more florid the emotional display, the more, as readers, we are discouraged from seeking the reasons for such a display. Our clues reduced to a series of conventional gestures (screams, shudders, faints, sighs), we are virtually prevented from developing anything more than a programmed response to stock Gothic situations. The satirical portrait, common in the criticism of the period, of two novel-reading ladies at the circulating library points to the (ironically) ineffective result of what appear to be situations calling for maximal emotional response:

'My dear Laura, have you read the new novel I recommended to you, The Animated Skeleton? I assure you it is the production of a very

[54] Ibid., 15–16. [55] *Castle of Wolfenbach*, p. 64. [56] Ibid., 10.
[57] *The Castle of Otranto*, p. 103.

young lady, and is her first appearance in that character.'—*L.* 'Heaven grant it may be her last! What, a young lady in the character of an animated skeleton? I protest I shudder at the bare idea.'—'Pooh! You will know better soon! To be sure they used to frighten me a little at first, but it is nothing when you are used to it; there is nothing else read now, and for my part I would not give a farthing for a novel that had not something about ghosts, and skeletons, and hobgoblins, and Emily walking alone with a great lamp in her hand through a parcel of damp cellars, in search of something to terrify her to her heart's content.'[58]

In view of this kind of character (and reader) impoverishment, it becomes increasingly difficult to justify the application of such concepts as 'psychic archives'[59] or 'disintegration of identity'[60] to Gothic fiction, for both these terms assume a depth of personality that characters in such works almost consistently lack. Indeed, in the early Gothic in particular, characters are systematically sacrificed to other, more highly valued, aspects of narrative such as moral or plot. This subordination of character in Gothic fiction recurs frequently enough to cast doubt on recent critical celebrations of the Gothic as psychologically exploratory. The extent to which Gothic writers willingly analyse their characters obviously differs—Radcliffe's treatment of Schedoni in *The Italian* or Lewis's of Ambrosio in *The Monk* are obviously more complex—but it is one of the more perplexing and interesting characteristics of Gothic fiction that its practitioners become adept at retreating from a full exploration of the characters they create. Even in the case of Radcliffe's Schedoni or Lewis's Ambrosio, the villains lose much of their vitality by the end of the novel: Schedoni, in murdering Nicola, commits a revenge so horrible that it eliminates any trace of sympathy we might have had for him, and Ambrosio, like Victoria in Charlotte Dacre's *Zofloya*, is impoverished by his author's refusal to come to terms with his temptations as human ones. Like Dacre, Lewis at the close reveals the tempter to be Satan in disguise.

[58] 'Modern Literature', *Aberdeen Magazine: or, Universal Repository*, iii (1798), 339. Jane Austen's Catherine Morland and Isabella Thorpe delight themselves in a similar way with their 'horrid' novels in *Northanger Abbey*.

[59] J. E. Hogle, 'The Restless Labyrinth: Cryptonymy in the Gothic Novel', *Arizona Quarterley*, xxxvi (1980), 332.

[60] Howells, *Love, Mystery, and Misery*, p. 30.

Particularization of character is rare, which is why, in Sedgwick's view, there tends to be 'unbounded confusion along the diacritical axes'; most Gothic villains look alike and virtually all Gothic heroines do. Indeed, in an interesting, though understandable, slip of priorities, the real heroes of the Gothic may be, as Maurice Lévy has suggested, and as many titles of Gothic novels confirm, not people at all but buildings: the novelists' failure to explore internal psychological spaces is often more than compensated for by an intense interest in setting.[61]

Characters in the Gothic are often, in fact, so highly generalized or idealized that no truly individual portraits emerge at all. Sir Philip, in Reeve's *Old English Baron,* is an example of such a figure. His reaction to the death of his friend, Lord Lovel ('The will of heaven be obeyed!'),[62] is so impersonal and formulaic that we cease to be aware of him as a personality; he becomes, rather, a commentator on actions that are being performed by others.

Scott noted a similar subordination of character to scene in the work of Ann Radcliffe, commenting that the force of her production lay in 'the delineation of external incident' and not in character.[63] Characters, indeed, are often lost sight of in moments of marked scenic intensity in Radcliffe's fiction. Her heroines respond to Alpine scenery with the same enthusiastic awe whatever their circumstances: even Ellena, as she is being abducted through the machinations of the Marchesa di Vivaldi, temporarily forgets her misfortunes in the face of a glorious mountain pass.[64]

This same quick sacrifice of character may also occur as a response to the demands of plot. In such instances, characters will suddenly exhibit behaviour that has no relationship to their previous actions. Walpole's *Castle of Otranto* contains

[61] M. Lévy, *Le Roman 'gothique' anglais 1764–1824,* Publications de la Faculté des Lettres et Sciences Humaines de Toulouse, sér. A, t. 9 (Toulouse, 1968), 268–74.

[62] *The Old English Baron,* p. 10.

[63] [Sir Walter Scott], 'Prefatory Memoir to Mrs Ann Radcliffe', in *The Novels of Mrs Ann Radcliffe,* Ballantyne's Novelist's Library, x (London, 1824), xviii. For a recent discussion of the role of landscape in Radcliffe's fiction (and its association with the delineation of character), see Daniel Cottom, *The Civilized Imagination: A Study of Ann Radcliffe, Jane Austen, and Sir Walter Scott* (Cambridge, 1985), pp. 35–50.

[64] *The Italian,* p. 63.

two such figures: Isabella's father, Frederic, who has not shown significant signs of weakness since his introduction in the novel, wavers in his mission in order to complicate the plot and increase the possibilities of Manfred's union with the heroine. Manfred himself repeatedly becomes sensitive when the plot requires it, when a period of respite is needed for Isabella, or when Walpole wants to strengthen the impact of a pathetic scene. In *The Mysteries of Udolpho*, Emily resists the evil reports of Montoni's character with a *naïveté* she exhibits nowhere else in the novel. Rosalina demonstrates the same unnatural stubbornness in *Manfroné*, refusing to leave a father who has imprisoned both her and her lover in a gloomy dungeon and is trying to force her into marriage with the hated and unprincipled Manfroné. (Rosalina's father later attempts her life with a dagger.) In Parsons's *Castle of Wolfenbach*, a previously gentle and benevolent character, Mrs Courtney, becomes increasingly and unusually jealous over the Count's affection for Matilda and tries to alienate the two, telling Matilda of the Count's attentions towards herself.[65] In each of these cases, the desire for a more extended or complicated plot outweighs the sense that character should be consistent (or believable). The degree to which plot exercises pressure upon characters in the Gothic becomes most noticeable in instances like these, or at the conclusions of novels where heretofore complex characters, like La Motte or Schedoni, undergo the radical simplification that is necessary to conclude the novel neatly and justly. The more elaborate the plot, the more disposable the characters: the story of Regina Maria Roche's *Clermont* is so exceedingly complicated and based to such a degree on concealment and mystery that it is virtually impossible for her to develop more than a few characters in any detail, and the plot (one of treachery between brothers, fathers, sons, and between husbands and wives) is set in motion by a character —D'Alembert—whom we do not even actually meet until very near the novel's end. The psychological motivations for the tale, thus, as a partial consequence, remain an almost total mystery until the last volume, whereupon all is unravelled, almost exclusively through second-hand accounts of the action.

[65] *Castle of Wolfenbach*, p. 115.

EFFECT AND CAUSE

The dominance accorded scene, plot, and device in Gothic narrative imposes limitations on character and poses other, equally troubling, problems of interpretation. In the works of Walpole and Beckford, in particular, many properties or objects that appear to have symbolic qualities are found ultimately to be completely lacking in significant resonance. Thus, as Kiely argues, the helmet and sword of *The Castle of Otranto*, because of a reduction of meaning in other parts of the narrative, do not function as true symbols; they are 'not phallic symbols because the characters have no lives to which they can refer'.[66] The Gothic, indeed, repeatedly fails to operate on this more complex double level of significance. Symbolic equivalences or parallels are discouraged because they are supported on no other plane of the narrative. Thus, Julia's flight through the underground passages in *A Sicilian Romance* is not a descent into her subconscious because Radcliffe retreats throughout the novel from deepening character by posing specific analogues between personality and setting. The imagery in that section, indeed, leads us doggedly back to the surface, to the extent that the sequence unintentionally acquires the qualities of near slapstick:

> They *entered* the avenue, and locking the door after them, sought the flight of steps *down* which the count had before passed . . . They *now entered* upon a dark abyss; and the door which moved upon a spring, suddenly *closed* upon them. On *looking round* they beheld a large vault; and it is not easy to imagine their horror on discovering they were in a receptacle for the murdered bodies of the unfortunate people who had fallen into the hands of the banditti. . . .
>
> They had not been long in this situation, when they heard a noise which *approached gradually*, and which did not appear to come *from the avenue* they had passed.

[66] R. Kiely, *The Romantic Novel in England* (Cambridge, Mass., 1972), p. 41. Cf. W. Raleigh, *The English Novel* (London, 1894), p. 223: 'The tricks and fantasies of supernaturalism are meaningless and powerless save in alliance with the mysterious powers of human nature, and, failing this, not all the realistic circumstance in the world can give them life or meaning.' Walpole, interestingly, seems to stress (and enjoy) this gap between sign and meaning in his account of the composition of *The Castle of Otranto:* one morning he dreamt of a gigantic hand in armour; that evening he 'sat down, and began to write, without knowing in the least what I intended to say . . .' (Walpole to the Revd William Cole, 9 Mar. 1765, *Correspondence*, i. 88).

. . . Hippolitus believed the murderers were *returned;* that they had traced his retreat, and were coming *towards the vault* by some way unknown to him. He prepared for the worst—and drawing his sword, resolved to defend Julia to the last. Their apprehension, however, was soon dissipated by a trampling of horses, which sound had occasioned his alarm, and which now seemed to come *from a courtyard above,* extremely *near the vault*. . . .

The tumult had continued a considerable time, which the prisoners had passed in a state of *horrible suspence,* when they heard the uproar advancing *towards the vault* . . . Hippolitus again drew his sword, and placed himself *opposite the entrance*, where he had *not stood* long, when a violent push was made against the door; it flew open, and a party of men rushed *into the vault.*

. . . the men *before him* were not banditti, but the officers of justice. . . .

Hippolitus enquired for Ferdinand, and they all *quitted the vault* in search of him. . . .

. . . On close examination [of the room in which Hippolitus had seen the dying cavalier], they perceived . . . a trap-door, which with some difficulty they lifted . . . They all *descended* . . . [67]

This passage gains its effect from its precise delineation of physical space, not from its description of emotional response: Hippolitus and Julia register only the conventional emotions of 'horror' and 'horrible suspence'; Hippolitus, preparing 'for the worst', draws his sword and resolves 'to defend Julia to the last'. The unease in the situation appears to arise from the constantly shifting perimeters of space that surround them and which they traverse: they descend steps, enter an abyss, look around; noises approach from other avenues, from above; they leave the vault; then they all descend.

The amount of movement here is so obviously exaggerated that it impedes a reflective response on the part of the reader, a response of the kind that Maturin, in a similar section in *Melmoth the Wanderer,* clearly invites. The scene is Monçada's underground flight with the parricide. With its syntactic repetitions ('I listen. . . I speak to you. . . I hate. . . I dread you') and its emphasis on strong emotion, the passage gains a horrifying power that is missing from Radcliffe's drama:

[67] *A Sicilian Romance*, ii. 138–46; emphasis added.

'Though my blood [Monçada says to the parricide], *chilled* as it is by *famine and fatigue,* seems *frozen* in every drop while I *listen* to you, yet *listen* I must, and trust my *life and liberation* to you. *I speak to you* with the horrid confidence our situation has taught me,— *I hate,—I dread you. If we were to meet in life, I would shrink* from you with loathings of unspeakable abhorrence, *but here* mutual misery has mixed the most repugnant susbstances in unnatural coalition. The force of that alchemy must cease at the moment of my escape *from the convent and from you;* yet, for these miserable hours, *my life is as much dependent* on your exertions and presence, *as my power of supporting them is* on the continuance of your horrible tale . . .'[68]

A tendency to tease the reader with effects is characteristic, especially, of the early Gothic and has misled many modern critics of the form: the genre's preoccupation with subterranean settings does not, in contrast to what some commentators have hopefully argued, necessarily point to a concern with human psychology, female physiology, or the unconscious. The genre, indeed, repeatedly fails to engage these deeper issues, and its failure involves a complex inability to confront both moral and aesthetic responsibilities: its often feverish search after sensation is puzzlingly joined with a deliberate retreat from meaning. This paradox is also the central one of the picturesque (and one about which Ruskin was particularly concerned). It is only by neatly (and naïvely) disjoining cause and effect that Gilpin, for example, can assert that Cromwell and Henry VIII were 'masters of ruins'[69] or that trees with disease are often pictorially more desirable than healthy ones, 'capital sources of picturesque beauty'.[70] Effect in such instances not only outweighs cause; it becomes a substitute for it, an excuse for not exploring more deeply the moral implications of a scene. Gilpin alludes periodically to this tension between aesthetic and moral categories, to the fact that, as he put it in *Cumberland,* 'moral, and picturesque ideas do not

[68] *Melmoth the Wanderer,* p. 209; emphasis added.

[69] William Gilpin, *Observations, Relative Chiefly to Picturesque Beauty, Made in the Year 1772, On Several Parts of England; Particularly the Mountains, and Lakes of Cumberland, and Westmoreland* (2 vols., London, 1786), ii. 122–3.

[70] William Gilpin, *Remarks on Forest Scenery, and Other Woodland Views, (Relative Chiefly to Picturesque Beauty) Illustrated by the Scenes of New-Forest in Hampshire. In Three Books* (2 vols., London, 1791), i. 8.

always coincide',[71] but he was reluctant to examine this interesting observation in any real detail.

Gothic novelists in a similar way often betray an attitude towards experience that emphasizes a disjunctive relationship between aesthetic and moral values. Radcliffe, whose theological distaste for Catholicism was acute, repeatedly uses Catholic settings in her novels, and on her journey through the Lake District in 1794, sought out and enjoyed scenes of lost Catholic splendour. '[T]hough reason rejoices that they no longer exist,' she remarked on the ruined monasteries on her tour, 'the eye may be allowed to regret'.[72] Walpole's response (around the time of *Otranto*) to the news of a large wolf that had caused devastation in Languedoc suggests a similar inclination to evade the actual in favour of the ideal: if he had known about it earlier, he said, he might have included it in *The Castle of Otranto*.[73] Beckford's reaction to the collapse of his tower at Fonthill shows a like self-absorbed disregard for practical consequences: he reported himself disappointed to have missed the spectacle. Distance, indeed, is a condition of aesthetic experience for Beckford: his travel diaries seldom contain direct observations about the towns he is visiting; instead, he coyly describes Flanders in Grecian terms, and Rome as if he were in Africa. He created another protective triangle in his relationship with Kitty Courtenay and Louisa Beckford, using Louisa, who loved him, as a shield for his correspondence with Kitty, with whom he was enamoured. This triangulating pattern marks all the major projects of Beckford's literary and personal life, allowing him the luxury of elaborate displays of wit without necessitating a close or spontaneous approach to his subject.

[71] *Observations . . . On Several Parts of England; Particularly the Mountains, and Lakes of Cumberland, and Westmoreland*, ii. 44.

[72] Ann Radcliffe, *A Journey Made in the Summer of 1794, through Holland and the Western Frontier of Germany, With a Return Down the Rhine: To Which are added Observations During a Tour to the Lakes of Lancashire, Westmoreland, and Cumberland*, 2nd edn. (2 vols., London, 1796), ii. 250.

[73] Walpole to Hertford, 26 Mar. 1765, *Correspondence*, xxxviii. 525.

EMOTION

Such emphases on emotional displays and effects (often to the exclusion of causes) are complicated further by the distrust some Gothic writers display about emotion itself. In *The Mysteries of Udolpho,* the work in which Radcliffe seems most fully aware of the destructive side of the sensitivity with which her heroines are endowed, St Aubert utters his famous warning to Emily:

'Above all, my dear Emily . . . do not indulge in the pride of fine feeling, the romantic error of amiable minds. Those, who really possess sensibility, ought early to be taught, that it is a dangerous quality, which is continually extracting the excess of misery, or delight, from every surrounding circumstance. And, since, in our passage through this world, painful circumstances occur more frequently than pleasing ones, and since our sense of evil is, I fear, more acute than our sense of good, we become the victims of our feelings, unless we can in some degree command them. . . .

. . . Always remember how much more valuable is the strength of fortitude, than the grace of sensibility. . . . Sentiment is a disgrace, instead of an ornament, unless it leads us to good actions. . . .'[74]

His reservations are echoed throughout the novel, most particularly by the straightforward Theresa:

'Dear dear! to see how some people fling away their happiness, and then cry and lament about it, just as if it was not their own doing, and as if there was more pleasure in wailing and weeping, than in being at peace. Learning, to be sure, is a fine thing, but, if it teaches folks no better than that, why I had rather be without it; if it would teach them to be happier, I would say something to it, then it would be learning and wisdom too.'[75]

Radcliffe's insistence that her heroines display fortitude and withstand prolonged suffering has an interesting effect on our apprehension of the value she accorded emotion. As the example of the nun Agnes shows, and as the fate of many other high-tempered Gothic females such as Dacre's Victoria corroborates, the relinquishment of the self to passion is not intrinsically good:

'Sister! beware of the first indulgence of the passions; beware of the first! Their course, if not checked then, is rapid—their force is

[74] *The Mysteries of Udolpho,* pp. 79–80. [75] Ibid., 637.

uncontroulable—they lead us we know not whither—they lead us perhaps to the commission of crimes, for which whole years of prayer and penitence cannot atone!—Such may be the force of even a single passion, that it overcomes every other, and sears up every other approach to the heart. Possessing us like a fiend, it leads us on to the acts of a fiend, making us insensible to pity and to conscience. And, when its purpose is accomplished, like a fiend, it leaves us to the torture of those feelings, which its power had suspended—not annihilated,—to the tortures of compassion, remorse, and conscience. . . . Remember, sister, that the passions are the seeds of vices as well as of virtues, from which either may spring, accordingly as they are nurtured. Unhappy they who have never been taught the art to govern them!'[76]

Agnes's warning about the ungovernability of the passions is one that is reiterated throughout the Gothic: sensibility, it is stressed, is a particularly volatile quality that can easily become destructive.[77] The Gothic heroine's job, then, seems to call into question the very novel that engendered her. Endowed with the sensitivity to be moved by the events around her, she must also, importantly, strive to resist their effects. It is thus not surprising to find that Radcliffe's heroines have a tendency to speak of their feelings in terms of restraint: 'Recollecting that she had parted with Valancourt, perhaps for ever, her heart sickened as memory revived. But she tried to dismiss the dismal forebodings that crowded on her mind, and to restrain the sorrow which she could not subdue; efforts which diffused over the settled melancholy of her countenance an expression of tempered resignation, as a thin veil, thrown over the features of beauty, renders them more interesting by a partial concealment.'[78] The virtuous Matilda in *The Castles of Athlin and Dunbayne* is similarly admired for what she holds herself from doing: 'Overwhelmed by the news, and deprived of those numbers which would make revenge successful, Matilda forbore to sacrifice the lives of her few remaining people to a

[76] Ibid., 646–7.

[77] For more on Radcliffe's distrust of sensibility (a stance that seems to contradict one of the fundamental premises of her art), see N. C. Smith, 'Sense, Sensibility and Ann Radcliffe', *Studies in English Literature*, xiii (1973), 577–90.

[78] *The Mysteries of Udolpho*, p. 161.

feeble attempt at retaliation, and she was constrained to endure in silence her sorrows and her injuries.'[79] This linking of heroism with restraint poses some serious problems for Gothic narrative. As Radcliffe's heroines are allowed less access to their emotions, they become systematically less complex—more 'flat', more passive, and more reliant upon other characters (like Schedoni or Montoni) to provide a balanced dispersal of emotional energies within the narratives in which they act. This attempt to achieve balance, however, is rarely successful in Gothic fiction. The insistent internalizing of passion on the part of Radcliffe's heroines—and the author's ambivalent attitude towards the emotions—marks the movement of Radcliffean Gothic as one of repeated suppression and repression: events are withstood, secrets are internalized, fears remain unvoiced. A seeming attempt to stabilize here ranges strangely out of control: to try to govern, or suppress, the passions may lead to fixation (Emily looking at the corpse) or physical collapse (Emily at the veiled portrait).

The achievement of stabilization, or closure, in the Gothic thus becomes a curiously two-sided enterprise: desired because of its connections with resolution and the conquest of good over evil, it is nonetheless increasingly seen as an inadequate, or unrealistic, response to the pressures of passion and vice. Many illustrations of Gothic fiction seem (perhaps unconsciously) to stress this aspect of the mode: capturing the frozen gestures of astonishment on the part of the virtuous characters, they repeatedly display the helpless fixation or fainting away of women unable any longer to contain their physical or emotional responses to the evil that faces them. It is not until later, in the more psychologically complex works of William Godwin, James Hogg, and Mary Shelley, that this urge towards stabilization is relinquished in any comfortable way; no longer concerned with imposing a predetermined moral and structural order on the experiences they relate, their works gain a coherence, a sustained unity of tone that much earlier Gothic fiction lacks.

[79] *The Castles of Athlin and Dunbayne*, p. 3.

2 *Techniques of Destabilization and Excess*

If the conventions of Gothic narrative that are designed to provide a comforting link to older fiction and older, moral themes—the tendency to anchor the fiction in a real, historical past, the inclination to 'flatten' character to produce a more simply balanced ethical tale, the use of coincidence to hint at a providentially superintended universe—often appear to be sources of problems rather than coherent stabilizing points within the stories (and hence disrupt the novels unintentionally), other techniques of the Gothic function deliberately to create an atmosphere of unease that is directly conducive to the 'Gothic' mood of fearful suspense. The result is a form of writing—and an experience of reading—that is essentially disruptive and subversive (though not always intentionally so). Part of the distinctive experience of the Gothic may actually derive from the reader's unconscious displeasure at the conjunction of these two structural modes: with its characteristic pattern of alternating static moralizing passages with scenes of often hectic action, it seems to demand an activity of consolidating on the part of its readership that its own design subverts. The result is a form that is fundamentally unstable, both in theory and in practice.

In 1800, the Marquis de Sade suggested a direct link between the instability of the Gothic form and the revolutionary turmoil of Europe: 'Pour qui connaissait tous les malheurs dont les méchans peuvent accabler les hommes, le Roman devenait aussi difficile à faire, que monotone à lire . . . il fallait donc appeller l'enfer à son secours, pour se composer des titres à l'intérêt, et trouver dans le pays des chimères, ce qu'on savait couramment en ne fouillant que l'histoire de l'homme dans cet âge de fer.'[1] It is difficult to say in what degree the Gothic novel

[1] D. A. F., Marquis de Sade, *Idée sur les romans,* ed. O. Uzanne (Paris, 1878), pp. 32–3. André Breton and Michael Sadleir, among others, share this view. See Breton, 'Limites non frontières du surréalisme', *Nouvelle revue française,* xlviii (1937), 210; Sadleir, *The Northanger Novels: A Footnote to Jane Austen,* English Association Pamphlet no. 68 (November, 1927) (Oxford, 1927), p. 7. An interesting contemporary review links the two revolutions explicitly: 'A Jacobin Novelist' [Letter to the editor], in the *Monthly Magazine,* iv (1798), 102–4.

is a response to the doubts and fears of the French Revolution (or even, as Lévy posits, of the Revolution of 1688).[2] Ronald Paulson has recently argued persuasively that its conventions—battlemented castles, tyrannical overseers, and heroines in distress—speak directly to English anxieties about the war.[3] The form, certainly, is centrally concerned with problems of power, authority, and institutional (especially Catholic) oppression,[4] and its efforts to stabilize itself often fail in puzzling and complex ways. In refusing, however, to confront these issues directly (for the form bears little resemblance to the doctrinal novels of the same period),[5] the genre often, as André Breton realized, takes on an opposite, 'precious' quality, an aura of distance and a mystique that excuse it from engaging in issues of political moment. Walpole's view of the Gothic was essentially of this 'insulating', protective kind. 'I almost think', he wrote in 1766, 'there is no wisdom comparable to that of exchanging what is called the realities of life for dreams. Old castles, old pictures, old histories . . . make one live back in centuries that cannot disappoint one. One holds fast and surely what is past. The dead have exhausted their power of deceiving—one can trust Catherine of Medicis now.'[6] *The Castle of Otranto*, indeed, was written in a deliberate attempt to escape from the political frenzy of the moment—'[A]dd', said Walpole to Cole, 'that I was very glad to think of anything rather than politics'[7]—(though whether that turmoil is

[2] M. Lévy, *Le Roman 'gothique' anglais 1764–1824*, Publications de la Faculté des Lettres et Sciences Humaines de Toulouse, sér. A, t. 9 (Toulouse, 1968), 613–15.

[3] R. Paulson, *Representations of Revolution (1789–1820)* (New Haven, 1983), pp. 215–47.

[4] See M. M. Tarr, *Catholicism in Gothic Fiction: A Study of the Nature and Function of Catholic Materials in Gothic Fiction in England* (Washington, DC, 1946).

[5] On the English novel of intention, see G. Kelly, *The English Jacobin Novel 1780–1805* (Oxford, 1976). The free uses to which history is put in most Gothic narrative suggest the writers' tendency to discount the factual or political contributions of their novels in favour of effect. As Sophia Lee remarks in the Advertisement to her *Recess*, 'the reign of Elizabeth was that of romance. If this Lady was not the child of fancy, her fate can hardly be paralleled; and the line of which she came has been marked by an eminent historian, as one distinguished by splendid misery' (i. vii). Mary Meeke, more dramatically, in *Count St. Blancard* (1795), wrote of contemporary France as if the Revolution had never taken place.

[6] Walpole to George Montagu, 5 Jan. 1766, *Correspondence*, x. 192.

[7] Walpole to the Revd William Cole, 9 Mar. 1765, *Correspondence*, i. 88.

successfully avoided is open to debate). Hence, the setting Breton imagines for his spree of Gothic novel reading in *Les Vases communicants* is delicately artificial and sealed off from the real world. In his little library with Gothic windows, he describes the experience of reading writers like Ann Radcliffe, whom Walter Raleigh once described as completely ignorant of the world:[8]

> Je supputai l'effet que ces petits volumes, dans leur charmante reliure Directoire ou sous leur couverture d'un bleu ou d'un rose uni un peu fané, ne pouvaient manquer de produire pour peu qu'on leur ménageât cette présentation. D'autre part ces livres étaient tels qu'on pouvait les prendre et les ouvrir au hasard, il continuait à s'en dégager on ne sait quel parfum de forêt sombre et de hautes voûtes. Leurs héroïnes, mal dessinées, étaient impeccablement belles. Il fallait les voir sur les vignettes, en proie aux apparitions glaçantes, toutes blanches dans les caveaux. Rien de plus excitant que cette littérature ultra-romanesque, archi-sophistiquée. Tous ces châteaux d'Otrante, d'Udolphe, des Pyrénées, de Lovel, d'Athlin et de Dunbayne, parcourus par les grandes lézardes et rongés par les souterrains, dans le coin le plus enténébré de mon esprit persistaient à vivre de leur vie factice, à présenter leur curieuse phosphorescence.[9]

Breton's expressions of pleasure—like those of an earlier reviewer of *The Mysteries of Udolpho*—are directed towards a combination of emotions that is uniquely Gothic: a mixture of terror, artifice, and luxury—in William Enfield's words, a 'strange luxury of artificial terror'.[10] This interesting complex of feelings is often heightened in the Gothic in moments of moral and spiritual decay, or of vulnerability and threat, and there is a tendency for many Gothic novelists to fix such scenes pictorially and linger over them. Maturin, describing the appearance of the suffering Walberg family or the flaying of an

[8] W. Raleigh, *The English Novel, Being a Short Sketch of its History from the Earliest Times to the Appearance of* Waverley (London, 1894), p. 228: 'Her ignorance of the world at the time when she wrote was complete and many-sided. Human character she knew, not from observation but from dreams. The landscapes for which she is so justly famous are pictures of countries she never saw. There is nothing in her books that she did not create. And it is a testimony to the power of her art that her fancy first conceived a type of character that subsequently passed from art into life. The man that Lord Byron tried to be was the invention of Mrs. Radcliffe.'

[9] A. Breton, *Les Vases communicants* (Paris, 1955), p. 134.

[10] *Monthly Review*, 2nd ser., xv (1794), 280.

innocent novitiate, and Radcliffe, picturing Ferdinand suspended on a crumbling staircase in *A Sicilian Romance*, or pausing over the burial of Madame Montoni, are concerned not simply with the fixation of fear but the strangely compelling, luxurious quality of decay. As Maturin put it in *The Milesian Chief*, a 'mixture of deviation and decay . . . combines our admiration of greatness with our interest in debility'.[11] This mingling of awe and horrified fascination is shown clearly in the scene in *Melmoth the Wanderer* in which Ines, the mother of the starving Walberg family, discovers that her eldest son has been selling his blood to a surgeon to keep his family from perishing:

> The moon-light fell strongly through the unshuttered windows on the wretched closet that just contained the bed. Its furniture was sufficiently scanty, and in his spasms Everhard had thrown off the sheet. So he lay, as Ines approached his bed, in a kind of corse-like beauty, to which the light of the moon gave an effect that would have rendered the figure worthy the pencil of a Murillo, a Rosa, or any of those painters, who, inspired by the genius of suffering, delight in representing the most exquisite of human forms in the extremity of human agony. A St Bartholomew flayed, with his skin hanging about him in graceful drapery—a St Laurence, broiled on a gridiron, and exhibiting his finely-formed anatomy on its bars, while naked slaves are blowing the coals beneath it,—even these were inferior to the form half-veiled,—half-disclosed by the moon-light as it lay. The snow-white limbs of Everhard were extended as if for the inspection of a sculptor, and moveless, as if they were indeed what they resembled, in hue and symmetry, those of a marble statue. His arms were tossed above his head, and the blood was trickling fast from the opened veins of both,—his bright and curled hair was clotted with the red stream that flowed from his arms,—his lips were blue, and a faint and fainter moan issued from them as his mother hung over him.[12]

Although (as I have suggested in the previous chapter) the Gothic is in many important respects conventional and highly fixed in form, there appears among the writers of the genre not

[11] Charles Robert Maturin, *The Milesian Chief. A Romance* (4 vols. in 2, London, 1812; repr. 4 vols., New York, 1979), i. 11.

[12] Charles Robert Maturin, *Melmoth the Wanderer: A Tale*, ed. D. Grant (London, 1968), pp. 421–2.

only a certain distrust in the stability of the conventions that they use but a sense that stability itself is less interesting than moments of suspense or irresolution. Maturin's dwelling upon his portrait of Everhard in *Melmoth,* his precise attention to details of colour, shape, and position, and his delaying, through analogy, of the presentation of the actual scene suggest his own conviction that the picture is an evocative one. It is, indeed, the episodes of underground flight, the storms at sea, the 'trembl[ing] on the verge'[13] that energize Gothic narrative—not the moralizing conversations such as those between Ellena and Vivaldi. A certain poised instability is central to the establishment of the Gothic mood, to its fear and delight, to the 'pleasing dread' that forms the paradox of the Gothic response.

The artful disequilibrium of the Gothic is achieved in a number of ways. Not only do the Gothic writers make full conventional use of stylistic devices such as exaggeration, interruption, and fragmentation to destabilize their narratives; this stylistic instability is supplemented by a peculiar tonal imbalance as well as one that might be called modal or generic.[14] The effect of these distortions is a stylistic reproduction of paradox, of irregularity and decay that is akin to the aesthetic values of Price, Knight, and Gilpin, the main theoreticians of the picturesque.

THE KINETIC AND THE OBSCURE

William Gilpin, in his works on the Wye Valley and the Highlands of Scotland, wrote frequently of the keen aesthetic pleasure produced by sudden shifts of scenery, especially that involving light. In 1776, on his approach to Dunheld, he takes a road that winds in such a way that the scenery shifts rapidly before his eyes. 'There is something very amusing even in a hasty succession of beautiful scenes', he comments. 'The imagination is kept in a pleasing perturbation; while these floating, unconnected ideas become a kind of waking dream; and are often wrought up by fancy into more pleasing pictures; than

[13] *Milesian Chief,* i. iv–v.

[14] R. L. Platzner, ' "Gothic Versus Romantic": A Rejoinder', *PMLA* lxxxvi (1971), 266–7.

they in fact appear to be, when they are viewed with deliberate attention.'[15] Gilpin experiences a similar pleasure on the river Wye as the banks, folding over each other as the boat moves forward, interrupt and vary the view,[16] and in the seat of a chaise, where, again, rapid movement produces scenes that are 'like the visions of the imagination; or the brilliant landscapes of a dream'.[17] The Gothic speeds up these movements and pushes an essentially pleasurable experience into the realm of the disorienting. The final underground sequence in *A Sicilian Romance* is nearly kaleidoscopic in nature with the abrupt shifts in Julia's course as she heads (as she thinks) towards liberty, only to find banditti, as she escapes to what she fears will be imprisonment, instead to come upon the ministers of justice, who are themselves suddenly replaced by banditti. The involvement of light in such scenes sharpens the sense of pleasing anxiety. As Hippolitus leads Julia out of the underground passage, his light is nearly extinguished by a rush of air from a closed chamber; he is forced to put out his light while watching the banditti; finally, the light 'dawn[s] upon them' through the mouth of a cave which they traverse to reach the forest.[18]

The first scene of Radcliffe's *The Romance of the Forest* makes a similar use of light to disorient and distort. It takes place at night on a desolate heath with a gusting wind. The near absence of illumination is central to this picture: La Motte, approaching through darkness a light that is shining from an ancient cottage, is brought before a fire of dying embers—light is partial; outlines are blurred. This lack of light forces La Motte to gather most of his information auditorially, and what he hears terrifies him the more. Radcliffe's awareness of the picturesque and kinetic qualities of light leads her frequently to invent landscapes of striking luminous beauty, as a typical

[15] William Gilpin, *Observations, Relative Chiefly to Picturesque Beauty, Made in the Year 1776, On Several Parts of Great Britain; Particularly the High-Lands of Scotland* (2 vols., London, 1789), i. 112.

[16] William Gilpin, *Observations on the River Wye, and Several Parts of South Wales, &c. Relative Chiefly to Picturesque Beauty; Made in the Summer of the Year 1770*, 2nd edn. (London, 1789), p. 19.

[17] William Gilpin, *Remarks on Forest Scenery, and Other Woodland Views, (Relative Chiefly to Picturesque Beauty) Illustrated by the Scenes of New-Forest in Hampshire. In Three Books* (2 vols., London, 1791), ii. 225.

[18] Ann Radcliffe, *A Sicilian Romance*, new edn. (2 vols., London, 1821; repr. 2 vols. in 1, New York, 1972), ii. 148.

storm scene from *The Mysteries of Udolpho* shows:

While the lady abbess ordered refreshment, and conversed with the Countess, Blanche withdrew to a window, the lower panes of which, being without painting, allowed her to observe the progress of the storm over the Mediterranean, whose dark waves, that had so lately slept, now came boldly swelling, in long succession, to the shore, where they burst in white foam, and threw up a high spray over the rocks. A red sulphureous tint overspread the long line of clouds, that hung above the western horizon, beneath whose dark skirts the sun looking out, illumined the distant shores of Languedoc, as well as the tufted summits of the nearer woods, and shed a partial gleam on the western waves. The rest of the scene was in deep gloom, except where a sun-beam, darting between the clouds, glanced on the white wings of the sea-fowl, that circled high among them, or touched the swelling sail of a vessel, which was seen labouring in the storm.[19]

This subtle rendering of light is duplicated in *The Italian,* where a description of the volcano Vesuvius creates a different but equally evocative background, an eerie and sinister atmosphere suggestive of dangerously explosive energies: 'It was nearly midnight, and the stillness that reigned was rather soothed than interrupted by the gentle dashing of the waters of the bay below, and by the hollow murmurs of Vesuvius, which threw up, at intervals its sudden flame on the horizon; and then left it to darkness.'[20] Fundamentally different from Walpole's disjunctive scenes in *The Castle of Otranto*, where sudden entrances and exits, crowds and evacuations, produce a feeling of extreme unease in the reader, the most successful scenes in Radcliffe's novels utilize a technique of de-escalation, of fading, lingering, and blurring to create an uncertain atmosphere in which actions, emotions, and landscape blend together in an unprecedented way. In an early episode in *The Mysteries of Udolpho,* Emily, visiting her father's grave, parts from a nun who has offered to accompany her to the site:

'You will remember, sister,' said she, 'that in the east aisle, which you must pass, is a newly opened grave; hold the light to the ground, that you may not stumble over the loose earth.' Emily, thanking her

[19] Ann Radcliffe, *The Mysteries of Udolpho: A Romance,* ed. B. Dobrée (London, 1970), pp. 484–5.

[20] Ann Radcliffe, *The Italian or the Confessional of the Black Penitents: A Romance,* ed. F. Garber (London, 1968), pp. 10–11.

again, took the lamp, and, stepping into the church, sister Mariette departed. But Emily paused a moment at the door; a sudden fear came over her, and she returned to the foot of the stair-case, where, as she heard the steps of the nun ascending, and, while she held up the lamp, saw her black veil waving over the spiral balusters, she was tempted to call her back. While she hesitated, the veil disappeared, and, in the next moment, ashamed of her fears, she returned to the church. The cold air of the aisles chilled her, and their deep silence and extent, feebly shone upon by the moon-light, that streamed through a distant gothic window, would at any other time have awed her into superstition; now, grief occupied all her attention. She scarcely heard the whispering echoes of her own steps, or thought of the open grave, till she found herself almost on its brink. A friar of the convent had been buried there on the preceding evening, and, as she had sat alone in her chamber at twilight, she heard, at distance, the monks chanting the requiem for his soul. This brought freshly to her memory the circumstances of her father's death; and, as the voices, mingling with a low querulous peal of the organ, swelled faintly, gloomy and affecting visions had arisen upon her mind. Now she remembered them, and, turning aside to avoid the broken ground, these recollections made her pass on with quicker steps to the grave of St. Aubert, when in the moonlight, that fell athwart a remote part of the aisle, she thought she saw a shadow gliding between the pillars.[21]

The atmospheric success of this scene, in which the boundaries between what is known and what is unknown gradually dissolve, depends largely on Radcliffe's ability to interpose and finally, possibly, to confuse past and present. By emphasizing the simultaneity of movements through an abundance of present participles, Radcliffe calls into question the integrity of objects, sounds, and even actions.

This technique of blurring and partially obscuring is central to Radcliffe's scenic effects. 'To a warm imagination,' she wrote in *The Mysteries of Udolpho*, 'the dubious forms, that float, half veiled in darkness, afford a higher delight, than the most distinct scenery, that the sun can shew',[22] and she reiterated the observation in her posthumously published essay, 'On the Supernatural in Poetry': '[O]bscurity, or indistinctness . . . [leaves] the imagination to act upon the few hints

[21] *The Mysteries of Udolpho*, pp. 90–1.
[22] Ibid., 598–9.

that truth reveals to it . . . Obscurity leaves something for the imagination to exaggerate. . . .'[23] Such a conviction permeates the writings of the picturesque theorists. 'Grand effects', Gilpin remarks in his *Observations on the Western Parts of England*, '. . . may often be produced by, what may be called, *the scenery of vapour*':

Nothing offers so extensive a field to the fancy in *invented* scenes . . . It admits the painter to a participation with the poet in the use of the machinery of *uncertain forms;* to which both are indebted for their *sublimest images*. . . . The regions of sublimity are not peopled by *forms*, but *hints*; they are not enlightened by *sunshine,* but by *gleams* and *flashes*. . . . The ideas of *grace* and *beauty* are as much raised by leaving the image half immersed in obscurity, as the ideas of *terror*. Definition, which throws a light on philosophic truth, destroys at once the airy shapes of fiction. . . . It is by snatches only that you catch a glimpse of such beauties. Would you analyse them, the vision dissolves in the process; and disappears, like life pursued to its last retreat by the anatomist. You ruin the image by determining its form, and *identifying its tints.*[24]

Though some later Gothicists (like Maturin) would experiment with what was doubtful or indistinct in morals, in most cases in Radcliffe's works this interest in obscurity is restricted to scenery. The effect is to create a backdrop of uncertainty and suspense that generates a sense of elusive 'Gothic' fear.

ACCELERATION

Less subtle techniques of disorientation are used by other Gothic writers, such as Walpole and Shelley. Rapidity of movement, traditionally connected with magic and often associated with the sublime, is frequently introduced to suggest the presence of supernatural agents (as in the carriage ride of Raymond and the Bleeding Nun in *The Monk*), or simply to unseat the reader from the normal rhythms of his world. Walpole deliberately accelerates the pace of his *Castle of Otranto:* 'Never is the reader's attention relaxed', he notes in

[23] Ann Radcliffe, 'On the Supernatural in Poetry', *New Monthly Magazine,* xvi (1826), 150.

[24] William Gilpin, *Observations on the Western Parts of England, Relative Chiefly to Picturesque Beauty. To Which Are Added, A Few Remarks on the Picturesque Beauties of the Isle of Wight* (London, 1798), pp. 166–7.

the preface to the first edition. '. . . Terror, the author's principal engine, prevents the story from ever languishing; and it is so often contrasted by pity, that the mind is kept up in a constant vicissitude of interesting passions.'[25] The author of *Vathek* similarly compresses events to quicken the speed of his tale. Mary-Anne Radcliffe's *Manfroné* opens with an attempted rape, a battle, and the severing of a hand, and the chronological sequence of the narrative is carefully rearranged so that the novel may open with these scenes of action. Such acceleration, particularly when it is, as in *The Castle of Otranto*, combined with a lack of focus, has a peculiarly disorienting effect. In Robert Kiely's analysis,

> Walpole attempts to evoke emotional agitation by means of theatrical gesture and movement, but his mind tries to work from the outside in and he succeeds only in putting his characters through frantic exercises which have no correspondence with the pace of human emotion. In a typical passage, a character is discovered by a princess 'prostrate on his face before the altar'; the princess shrieks, 'concluding him dead.' 'Rising suddenly, his face bedewed with tears, he would have rushed from her presence,' but is prevailed upon to explain his 'posture,' after which 'bursting from her,' he hastens to his own apartment where he is 'accosted' by the prince, who invites him 'to waste some hours of the night in music and revelling.' Offended by such levity, he pushes him 'rudely' aside, and entering his chamber, flings the door 'intemperately' shut and bolts it. Enraged by such treatment, the prince withdraws and as he crosses the court, is met by 'the domestic he had planted at the convent as a spy.' This man, 'almost breathless with the haste he had made,' informs his lord that 'Theodore and some lady from the castle' are at that instant 'in private conference at the tomb of Alfonso in St. Nicholas's church.' . . . The plot is part obstacle course, part free-for-all, and part relay race in which the participants run through a cluttered labyrinth passing the baton to whomever they happen to meet.[26]

Far from lightening the impact of the story, as Hume has argued, this hectic pace of emotions and events lends an ominously anarchical quality to the narrative. The author

[25] Horace Walpole, *The Castle of Otranto: A Gothic Story,* ed. W. S. Lewis (London, 1969), p. 4.

[26] R. Kiely, *The Romantic Novel in England* (Cambridge, Mass., 1972), pp. 34–5.

seems reluctant to pause to analyse specific scenes or to relate characters' responses to a total emotional range. The reader thus may feel that he is being swept away by a narrative over which no one has any real control. The beginning of Shelley's *Zastrozzi* plunges the audience directly into a whirlwind of undirected malevolence that is profoundly disorienting in this way:

> Torn from the society of all he held dear on earth, the victim of secret enemies, and exiled from happiness, was the wretched Verezzi!
>
> All was quiet; a pitchy darkness involved the face of things, when, urged by fiercest revenge, Zastrozzi placed himself at the door of the inn where, undisturbed, Verezzi slept.
>
> Loudly he called the landlord. The landlord, to whom the bare name of Zastrozzi was terrible, trembling obeyed the summons.
>
> 'Thou knowest Verezzi the Italian? he lodges here.' 'He does,' answered the landlord.
>
> 'Him, then, have I devoted to destruction,' exclaimed Zastrozzi. 'Let Ugo and Bernardo follow you to his apartment; I will be with you to prevent mischief.'[27]

'Whirling', repeatedly the verb used in *Zastrozzi* to describe mental processes, embodies the quality of rapid and uncontrolled movement that both energizes and disturbs the normal process of Shelley's narrative. As Hazlitt argued about similar characteristics in Shelley's poetry, the effect of such violent disjointedness is effectively to obscure any possibility for a didactic message:

> The *Witch of Atlas*, the *Triumph of Life*, and *Marianne's Dream*, are rhapsodies or allegories of this description; full of fancy and of fire, with glowing allusions and wild machinery, but which it is difficult to read through, from the disjointedness of the materials, the incongruous metaphors and violent transitions, and of which, after reading them through, it is impossible, in most instances, to guess the drift or the moral. . . . life, death, genius, beauty, victory, earth, air,

[27] Percy Bysshe Shelley, *Zastrozzi: A Romance* (1810), in R. Ingpen and W. E. Peck (eds.), *The Complete Works of Percy Bysshe Shelley* (10 vols., London, 1926–30), v. 5.

ocean, the trophies of the past, the shadows of the world to come, are huddled together in a strange and hurried dance of words, and all that appears clear is the passion and paroxysm of thought of the poet's spirit.[28]

This doctrine of speed, with its associations with the irrational and the inspired, was occasionally evoked to characterize the process of Gothic composition as well. Both Walpole and Beckford circulated stories of their romances having been conceived in the heat of the moment: Walpole announced in conversation that he had finished his novel in eight days,[29] and Beckford once asserted that he had written *Vathek* in a 'fit [lasting] two days and a night'.[30] Contemporary critics of the Gothic regularly commented on this aspect of the novels, though generally for the purpose of suggesting that its readers, too obtuse (or jaded) to respond to the subtler charms of 'higher literature', required this repeated exposure to exciting and wonderful events to arouse their interest. As one reviewer for the *Analytical Review* commented,

The mind, as well as the body, loses it's sensibility, or to borrow a fashionable term, it's *excitability,* by the too frequent reiteration of similar impressions; whence it becomes, in both cases, necessary, in order to preserve the same degree of irritation, to be continually increasing the stimulating force. As in the use of strong liquors, the same tone of hilarity can only be kept up by perpetually increasing the quantity of vinous spirit; so, in providing the public with the gratifications of fancy, the works of fiction, that they may keep pace with the progress of fastidiousness in taste, must gradually ascend from the most simple exhibition of natural sentiments and passions, through every stage of splendid ornament, and wild extravagance. It is from this principle, that we account for the present daily increasing rage for novels addressed to the strong passions of wonder and terrour.[31]

[28] William Hazlitt, 'Shelley's Posthumous Poems', in *The Complete Works of William Hazlitt,* ed. P. P. Howe (21 vols., London, 1930–4), xvi. 273.

[29] J. Pinkerton, *Walpoliana* (2 vols., London, 1799), i. 22.

[30] Notation in his copy of Hon. Col. L. Stanhope's *Greece in 1823–24, with Reminiscences of Lord Byron* (1825), cited in *Catalogue of The Third Portion of the Beckford Library, Removed from Hamilton Palace* (London, 1883), item 2193, p. 155.

[31] Review of *Count Roderic's Castle; or, Gothic Times, a Tale,* in the *Analytical Review,* xx (1794), 488–9.

INTERRUPTION AND FRAGMENTATION

One consequence of an allegiance to a rapid or intensified sequence of events is that characters and scenes cannot always be allowed to develop through conventional channels: reflective or descriptive passages would slow the action of the narrative and interfere with the desired visceral response. There is thus in such novels an increased attention to interruption and fragmentation as devices to curtail length and move the story forward to create the general atmosphere of unease that characterizes the Gothic. Both Walpole and Radcliffe use the procedure: in *Otranto*, interruption is employed to jar the reader or to tantalize him with information known but not immediately divulged. Ann Radcliffe (paradoxically) uses interruption to attenuate, not to shorten the narrative, often withholding information for chapters at a time, prolonging a lingering (and sometimes nearly forgotten) sense of mystery and dread. The mystery of the veil in *Udolpho* is a well-known instance of this technique, as is the enigma of St. Aubert's relationship to the Marchioness de Villeroi. Walpole's acts of restraining or interrupting are more abrupt than those of Radcliffe, and his scenes take on a rhythm of wrenching and foreshortening remarkably akin to that of comic strips: 'unless—At that instant Bianca burst into the room, with a wildness in her look and gestures that spoke the utmost terror.'[32] The frustrating foreshortening of narrative at the death of the hermit and at the supposed death of Frederic, and the truncation of Father Jerome's relation to Theodore of the tale of Alfonso repeat the pattern of short and disjunctive scenes. The interrupted deathbed warning is a favourite situation in Gothic tales. In the second chapter of *Manfroné*, a dying servant delivers this disconcerting message: ' "The signora Rosalina has a secret enemy; bid her to beware of—of— —" Here, without allowing him to conclude the important information he was on the point of disclosing, death stopped his further speech, and the signor remained in uncertainty as to the person.'[33]

[32] *The Castle of Otranto*, p. 98.

[33] Mary-Anne Radcliffe, *Manfroné; or, The One-Handed Monk. A Romance*, 3rd edn. (4 vols., London, 1828; repr. 4 vols. in 2, New York, 1972), i. 34–5.

Closes of chapters and volumes are often marked by sudden and ominous shifts of action or tone. The first volume of Sophia Lee's *The Recess* ends in this fashion: ' "It is open, cried he in a transport of joy, come, my love, and let me assist you to enter."—He did so, but hardly was I within it, ere I found myself violently seized by several persons, who instantly stopping my mouth, deprived me of strength to cry out had heaven lent it me; but agony and horror so entirely overcame me, I sunk senseless in their arms.'[34] Repeated exposure to such abruptly terminated scenes has the effect of discouraging causal or sequential analysis, for although the information that is necessary to clarify such moments is often given at the work's end, there are usually insufficient clues at the time of the action to enable the reader to explain fully what is happening. A sensitive reader may feel that his reasoning and emotions have been exploited: challenged to react strongly to a mystery that he cannot solve and to characters that he does not fully know, his field of possible responses narrows to satirical detachment or uncritical emotional involvement.

A variation of this technique of interruption is that of fragmentation or diasparaction. Thomas McFarland has demonstrated the prominence of this procedure in the work of the Romantic poets; it is also a device that Sterne uses repeatedly to disrupt narrative sequence in *Tristram Shandy*. The Gothic novelists predictably make use of the procedure for purposes of suspense. Invariably, important manuscripts suddenly break off or become illegible in crucial places, or must be read in sections or in fragments. *Melmoth the Wanderer* is an account taken from a manuscript 'discoloured, obliterated, and mutilated beyond any that had ever before exercised the patience of a reader',[35] full of hiatuses and defects. In *The Romance of the Forest,* Adeline reads—in pieces—a similarly decayed manuscript that contains a description of the sufferings of her father.

An auditory version of such a fragmented document occurs in *Manfroné*, as Rosalina overhears parts of a suspicious

[34] Sophia Lee, *The Recess; or, A Tale of Other Times* (3 vols., London, 1783–5; repr. New York, 1972), i. 256.

[35] *Melmoth the Wanderer*, p. 28.

conversation between her father and Lupo the castellain as they pace the ramparts of the castle:

'Passing along the forest late one evening, I saw at no great distance the signora Rosalina and the young marchese in earnest converse; curious to know what was the subject, I concealed myself behind some thick underwood, and — —'

Here distance prevented Rosalina from hearing the remainder of Lupo's speech, and she was about to retire from the casement, when she thought she heard them returning.

'Tis very strange,' said the duca. 'Lupo, there is somewhat to be feared in this: mark me—Montalto must— —'

The concluding words of his speech were spoke in so low a tone, that Rosalina could not distinguish what was said. . . .

Greatly agitated, Rosalina leaned on the stone frame of the casement for support. She did not entertain a doubt but that some dark plan was in agitation which threatened her lover . . .[36]

In *The Mysteries of Udolpho,* the 'sentence of dreadful import' that Emily involuntarily reads as she removes St Aubert's papers from beneath the floor-boards to burn them works in a similar—but far more masterful—way to generate suspense about St Aubert's past. The negative judgement towards which Emily and the reader are impelled shows the danger of drawing conclusions from pieces of evidence of which the context is unknown. Radcliffe's restraint in this passage mirrors the difficulty of exercising this kind of judgemental control. Unlike the author of *Manfroné,* her refusal to be explicit about what Emily reads and the dramatic gesture of destroying the paper (and hence all hope of putting the sentence in context) result in a far more affecting scene:

she turned to the papers, though still with so little recollection, that her eyes involuntarily settled on the writing of some loose sheets, which lay open; and she was unconscious, that she was transgressing her father's strict injunction, till a sentence of dreadful import awakened her attention and her memory together. She hastily put the papers from her; but the words, which had roused equally her curiosity and terror, she could not dismiss from her thoughts. So powerfully had they affected her, that she even could not resolve to destroy the papers immediately; and the more she dwelt on the cir-

[36] *Manfroné,* i. 77–8.

cumstance, the more it inflamed her imagination. Urged by the most forcible, and apparently the most necessary, curiosity to enquire farther, concerning the terrible and mysterious subject, to which she had seen an allusion, she began to lament her promise to destroy the papers. For a moment, she even doubted, whether it could justly be obeyed, in contradiction to such reasons as there appeared to be for further information. But the delusion was momentary. . . .

Thus re-animated with a sense of her duty, she completed the triumph of integrity over temptation, more forcible than any she had ever known, and consigned the papers to the flames. Her eyes watched them as they slowly consumed, she shuddered at the recollection of the sentence she had just seen, and at the certainty, that the only opportunity of explaining it was then passing away for ever.[37]

The recurrence of such disrupted structures in Gothic narrative suggests an interest in asymmetry and incompleteness that is often recapitulated in the works' imagery. The emphasis on dismemberment (or 'disarmament') in *The Castle of Otranto* is a case in point. Diego and Jaquez's view of a foot and part of a leg in the castle chamber repeats the same emphasis on partial vision and fragmentation apparent in some of Bianca's and the crowd's exclamations: 'Oh, the helmet! the helmet!'; 'Oh! the hand! the giant! the hand!'.[38] A similar—more grisly—event provides a focus for Mary-Anne Radcliffe's *Manfroné*. Manfroné, caught at the point of attempting to rape Rosalina, has his hand severed by the sword of Rosalina's father. It lies unnoticed, bleeding on the floor, until it is discovered by Rosalina's servant Carletta, and thrown into Lake Abruzzo by the castellain. Later it washes up on shore and is by chance discovered by Manfroné and attached by him to the dagger that kills the duca. Finally it functions in a negative sense to reveal the identity of Grimaldi: his lack of a hand proves him to be Manfroné in disguise.

Often, this device of the lacuna, the missing part, assumes a more troubling significance. In the novels of Ann Radcliffe, in particular, seemingly important issues (most often those of

[37] *The Mysteries of Udolpho*, pp. 103–4. The fragment became, interestingly, a popular mode of presenting Gothic tales in the magazines: its curtailed length was both provocative and practical.

[38] *The Castle of Otranto*, pp. 33–4; 16; 98.

psychological weight) are occasionally introduced only to be abandoned before they are sufficiently investigated by the author. The description of Adeline's dreams in *The Romance of the Forest* typifies this strategy of aesthetic and psychological evasion. In her first dream, Adeline sees herself in a mirror, covered with wounds; later, she has recurring dreams about a dying man and a funeral attendant, both of whom threaten her in a physical or sexual way:

> She thought she was in a large old chamber belonging to the abbey, more ancient and desolate, though in part furnished, than any she had yet seen. It was strongly barricadoed, yet no person appeared. While she stood musing and surveying the apartment, she heard a low voice call her, and looking towards the place whence it came, she perceived by the dim light of a lamp a figure stretched on a bed that lay on the floor. The voice called again, and approaching the bed, she distinctly saw the features of a man who appeared to be dying. A ghastly paleness overspread his countenance, yet there was an expression of mildness and dignity in it, which strongly interested her.
>
> While she looked on him his features changed, and seemed convulsed in the agonies of death. The spectacle shocked her, and she started back; but he suddenly stretched forth his hand, and seizing her's, grasped it with violence; she struggled in terror to disengage herself, and again looking on his face, saw a man, who appeared to be about thirty, with the same features, but in full health and of a most benign countenance. He smiled tenderly upon her, and moved his lips, as if to speak, when the floor of the chamber suddenly opened, and he sunk from her view. The effort she made to save herself from following, awoke her.[39]

In her second dream of this series, a man clad in a black cloak leads her through a long passage to the foot of a staircase and then turns to pursue her. In the next dream, she approaches the same man and sees the dying chevalier of the first dream, whose side opens and emits a stream of blood that floods the whole chamber. The images of these dreams are powerful ones—Radcliffe calls them 'terrific'[40] and admits that Adeline is shocked by them—but the description of Adeline's response erases any possibility of their reference to a particularized or

[39] Ann Radcliffe, *The Romance of the Forest,* new edn. (3 vols., London, 1827; repr. New York, 1974), i. 238–9.

[40] Ibid., ii. 18.

individual condition: 'This dream had so strongly impressed her fancy, that it was some time before she could overcome the terror it occasioned, or even be perfectly convinced she was in her own apartment. At length, however, she composed herself to sleep; again she fell into a dream.'[41] The dreams here are evasively restricted in meaning: they are simply dreams of a mysterious death and some obscure villainy—the dying man of the first and third dreams is neither explicitly her father nor a chevalier—and function chiefly to heighten Adeline's suspicion about foul play at the abbey. Radcliffe's reluctance to explore more fully the psychological substratum of her work is also apparent in the sonnets of her early novels, which often break forth with an intensity absent in the tale's narrative sections. A striking example of such a piece is the 'storied sonnet' on the Alpine traveller that Emily composes in *The Mysteries of Udolpho:*

STORIED SONNET

The weary traveller, who, all night long,
Has climb'd among the Alps' tremendous steeps,
Skirting the pathless precipice, where throng
Wild forms of danger; as he onward creeps
If, chance, his anxious eye at distance sees
The mountain-shepherd's solitary home,
Peeping from forth the moon-illumin'd trees,
What sudden transports to his bosom come!
But, if between some hideous chasm yawn,
Where the cleft pine a doubtful bridge displays,
In dreadful silence, on the brink, forlorn
He stands, and views in the faint rays
Far, far below, the torrent's rising surge,
And listens to the wild impetuous roar;
Still eyes the depth, still shudders on the verge,
Fears to return, nor dares to venture o'er.
Desperate, at length the tottering plank he tries,
His weak steps slide, he shrieks, he sinks—he dies![42]

[41] Ibid., i. 239–40.
[42] *The Mysteries of Udolpho,* p. 165.

The oddness of such poems lies in the combination of their imaginative vigour and their utter lack of authorial commentary. As in the case of the dreams, the sonnet is clearly neither a direct explanation nor an explicit, controlled extension of Emily's state of mind.

OVERSTATEMENT, INTENSIFICATION, AND EXAGGERATION

At the opposite pole from fragmentation and incompletion is a technique of overstatement in the Gothic that exerts an equally destabilizing effect on the narrative. In his *Letters on Chivalry and Romance,* Richard Hurd had praised the medieval romance for its energy and extravagance, and eighteenth-century Gothic writers seized on these qualities to a degree that distinguished them from their predecessors.[43] Exaggerated language and events are particularly the province of the later Gothic novelists such as Lewis, Maturin, and Shelley. Maturin's heavy use of dashes and exclamation points pitches his language with unusual force, and his distinctive use of parallelism and syntactic repetition intensifies the effect of the incidents he describes. The scene in which Melmoth proclaims the terms of his marriage to Immalee is an example of the way Maturin's language, in being 'overspecified', pushes towards the verge of the unnamable:

> 'Look up,' said the stranger, while his own fixed and fearless eye seemed to return flash for flash to the baffled and insulted elements; 'Look up, and if you cannot resist the impulses of your heart, let me at least point out a fitter object for them. Love,' he cried, extending his arm towards the dim and troubled sky, 'love the storm in its might of destruction—seek alliance with those swift and perilous travellers of the groaning air,—the meteor that rends, and the thunder that shakes it! Court, for sheltering tenderness, those masses of dense and rolling cloud,—the baseless mountains of heaven! Woo the kisses of the fiery lightnings, to quench themselves on your smouldering bosom! Seek all that is terrible in nature for your companions and

[43] Richard Hurd, *Letters on Chivalry and Romance, with the Third Elizabethan Dialogue,* ed. and with an introd. by E. J. Morley (London, 1911), p. 170 and *passim.*

your lover! — woo them to burn and blast you — perish in their fierce embrace, and you will be happier, far happier, than if you lived in mine! *Lived!* — Oh who can be mine and live! Hear me, Immalee!' he cried, while he held her hands locked in his — while his eyes, rivetted on her, sent forth a light of intolerable lustre — while a new feeling of indefinite enthusiasm seemed for a moment to thrill his whole frame, and new-modulate the tone of his nature; 'Hear me! If you will be mine, it must be amid a scene like this for ever — amid fire and darkness — amid hatred and despair — amid——'[44]

Maturin's contemporary critics were acutely aware of what Thomas Noon Talfourd would later call his 'love of strength and novelty in thought and expression', for which, Talfourd noted, 'he appears willing to make any sacrifice'.[45] Maturin's urge to represent extremes dominates his writing, and is accomplished here by a fairly simple additive method: Maturin reiterates with a second adjective, noun, or verb a condition or quality of the first word that is close enough to give the reader the effect not of differentiation but of sameness, of intensification of a single quality. Thus, the sky is 'dim and troubled', the clouds 'dense and rolling', the elements will 'burn and blast' Immalee. Subtle distinctions are not desired so much as 'a sort of excited psychology, an exclamatory insistence on sensation and emotion'.[46] Maturin explicitly refers to this desire to intensify in his dedication to *The Milesian Chief*: 'If I possess any talent,' he declares, 'it is that of darkening the gloomy, and of deepening the sad; of painting life in extremes, and representing those struggles of passion when the soul trembles on the verge of the unlawful and the unhallowed.'[47] The structure of *Melmoth the Wanderer* recapitulates this pattern of doubling and intensification, each narrator relating an ominously similar tale of oppression, despair, and temptation.[48]

In *The Castle of Otranto,* Walpole utilizes this same technique of exaggeration on the imagistic level of the narrative,

[44] *Melmoth the Wanderer,* p. 322.

[45] 'Remarks on "Melmoth" ', *New Monthly Magazine, and Universal Register,* xiv. ii (1820), 663.

[46] Review of *Melmoth the Wanderer,* in the *Athenæum,* no. 3366 (1892), p. 561.

[47] *Milesian Chief,* i. iv–v.

[48] An excellent account of the structural and syntactical complexities of *Melmoth the Wanderer* appears in Linda Bayer-Berenbaum, *The Gothic Imagination: Expansion in Gothic Literature and Art* (Rutherford, NJ, 1982), pp. 75–106.

dealing repeatedly with enormous immobile objects (casque, sword, hand) that produce a sense of extreme claustrophobia and fear.[49] It is, in effect, a dream of grotesque disproportion that inspires the story at all, by Walpole's famous account: 'I waked one morning, in the beginning of last June from a dream, of which all I could recover was, that I had thought myself in an ancient castle . . . and that on the uppermost bannister of a great staircase I saw a gigantic hand in armour. In the evening I sat down and began to write, without knowing in the least what I intended to say or relate.'[50] As a result of this inspiration, Walpole's tale is crammed with objects of immense size: the helmet that falls to the ground on the third page of the story and dashes Conrad to pieces is 'an hundred times more large than any casque ever made for human being, and shaded with a proportionable quantity of black feathers.'[51]

One problem with this simple method of intensifying is that it can descend easily into the burlesque. Although in melodrama language may push towards excess to polarize ethical alternatives,[52] the effect in the Gothic is often an opposite one: a troubling evacuation of moral criteria.[53] Walpole's flippant tone in describing the composition of *Otranto* suggests his sense, perhaps, that the image of the hand was so sensational that it required little thought to develop a story around it, that the tale's stupendousness, in effect, would excuse any haste or thoughtlessness in the main design. Shelley's repeated use of superlatives in *Zastrozzi* (Zastrozzi is Verezzi's 'bitterest enemy'; he is 'enraged beyond measure'; he is 'the cause of all his misfortunes') leaves his reader overwhelmed with an excess he cannot feel; and it is, significantly, only a small step from such inflated emotionalism to the burlesque of *Vathek*. Here, expansion reaches ludicrous extremes. The Caliph's tower, built at the rate of one cubit a day, is then built two cubits higher

[49] Lévy cites other examples of giganticism in his *Le Roman 'gothique' anglais*, 415.

[50] Walpole to the Revd William Cole, 9 Mar. 1765, *Correspondence*, i. 88.

[51] *The Castle of Otranto*, p. 17.

[52] See P. Brooks, *The Melodramatic Imagination: Balzac, Henry James, Melodrama, and the Mode of Excess* (New Haven, 1976).

[53] David Morris applies this paradox to linguistic meaning in the Gothic, arguing that Walpole's garrulity in *The Castle of Otranto* leads, in the end, to a reduction of language (which Morris associates with the sublime). See D. B. Morris, 'Gothic Sublimity', *New Literary History*, xvi (1985), 313.

every night; his dinner consists of 300 dishes, of which on the day of the capture of the Giaour, he is able to eat only thirty-two. This obsessive attention to exaggeration played an active role in Beckford's life as well. 'Some people drink to forget their happiness', he wrote to his friend Franchi; 'I do not drink, I build.'[54] His constant enlargement of house and gardens at Fonthill and later at Bath testifies to his ability to put that philosophy into practice. As a public reminder of this attraction to the vast, he installed mirrors at Fonthill to increase his sense of space and stationed a dwarf at the door to emphasize the Abbey's extraordinary height. *Vathek* (especially in scenes such as that involving the Giaour, who is kicked, kicked again, and finally rolled like a ball through the city of Samarah) demonstrates that when no more exaggeration is possible, the only option remaining is self-satire. The violence that increases as *Vathek* draws to a close is partially a response to the moral untenability of this narrative stance. By reducing (or expanding) all to the level of spectacle, Beckford's tale (like his tower at Fonthill) can only bring more pleasure when it self-destructs.

TONAL AND GENERIC INCONGRUITIES

The Gothic repeatedly exhibits an uncertainty about its tone that becomes more pronounced as the genre develops, and exaggerated theatrical gestures or language may be attempts to compensate for such doubts. As far as the supernatural aspect of the narrative is concerned, however, such self-consciousness is peculiar, for, as Scott remarked in his introduction to *The Castle of Otranto*, 'the reader, who is required to admit the belief of supernatural interference, understands precisely what is demanded of him . . .'[55] In a situation of this kind, in which the reader is perhaps even more dependent than usual on the narrator (who is establishing special parameters for the real), evidence of narrative uncertainty or self-distrust can be

[54] William Beckford to Gregorio Fellipe Franchi, 17 Aug. 1812, in *Life at Fonthill, 1807–1822*, ed. B. Alexander (London, 1957), p. 128.

[55] [Sir Walter Scott], in his introd. to *The Castle of Otranto; A Gothic Story* (Edinburgh, 1811), pp. xxiv–xxv.

especially disruptive and disturbing. Both Lewis and Maturin adopt an attitude at the beginning of *The Monk* and *Melmoth the Wanderer* that challenges the very premises the reader is ready to accept. Ann Radcliffe is less overt about her scepticism, but she is careful (as many of her readers found to their displeasure)[56] to provide rational explanations for most of her mysteries and often engages in self-conscious disclaimers about the nature of any apparently supernatural or overly romantic events she describes. In *The Romance of the Forest,* she repeats twice that La Motte's experience is improbable and fit only for romance and on the rumour of the abbey being haunted, Louis delivers this unlikely remark: 'the marvellous is the delight of the vulgar . . . Thus people, who have few objects of real interest to engage their thoughts, conjure up for themselves imaginary ones'.[57] In asserting that there are distinctions between the spirit world as apprehended by servants and that experienced by persons of sensibility, Radcliffe cleverly ensures her own protection; she can at once curb her own imaginative flights (dampening them through comic deflation, as she often does by allowing serving maids to exhibit ludicrous degrees of fear) and suggest that spirits may be real. For, in associating himself with the oppressed and sensitive maiden (as opposed to the merely superstitious servant), the reader will realize that receptivity to supernatural powers is a mark not of ignorance but of emotional refinement. Radcliffe's double view thus shields her from the accusation of wilful *naïveté,* as it does the audience that reads her work. Lewis pushes this self-consciousness to an extreme in *The Monk* in the creation of Leonella and Jacintha: the latter believes that Elvira's ghost appears because she must pay penance for having eaten a chicken wing on Friday. In *Vathek,* an exaggerated consciousness of generic conventions results in a total breaking apart of the story. Beckford cannot (or will not) abandon

[56] Such readers included Anna Laetitia Barbauld, Scott, and Coleridge. The disproportion between cause and effect generated by natural explanations of the supernatural was often, in the critics' views, so extreme that they 'must disgust every reader much more than if he were left under the delusion of ascribing the whole to supernatural agency'. See [Sir Walter Scott], Review of *Fatal Revenge,* in the *Quarterly Review,* iii (1810), 344.

[57] *The Romance of the Forest,* i. 14; i. 17; i. 153–4.

himself to fantasy and his insistence on using the conventions of the genre only to mock them produces a tainted tale that epitomizes the limits of such generic self-consciousness.

The Gothic regards itself carefully because it does not entirely trust itself as a genre. As Scott pointed out in his introduction to *The Castle of Otranto,* Gothic writers tacitly ask that we dread those legends that, during the day, we treat with derision, and that we embrace a mode of experience that our conscious 'day-time' selves have rejected.[58] We can resolve such an apparent paradox by admitting either that there exists some direct relationship between our lives and Gothic art, or that the reading of Gothic fiction is purely an escapist enterprise, that relevance to 'real' life is tangential and that direct connections are few. The moral purpose of most eighteenth- and early nineteenth-century fiction made the latter stance an undesirable one to take, yet readers were equally unwilling to admit ghosts, tapestries, or medieval history into the realm of their public experience. This fragility of the Gothic is, in effect, what may account for the frequent moments of self-satire in the genre and for the proclivity of many romance writers to account for supposed supernatural events in rational ways (a tendency that may, as well, be interpreted as self-satiric).

Related to this atmosphere of tonal imbalance in the Gothic is a quality that Robert Platzner has called 'generic instability'.[59] In its reliance upon a mixture of genres (fairy tale, romance, Jacobean drama,[60] and novel of manners), the Gothic novel often contains unintentionally humorous instances of collision, in which the demands of one mode are brought up—sometimes startlingly—against the exigencies of another. The conflicting requirements of the providential and the romance forms are evident in *The Old English Baron;* in the works of Radcliffe and Walpole, the heroines' demure concern about escaping in the proper attire and in the proper way is a more obviously comic example of the novels' proneness towards

[58] [Scott], introd. to *The Castle of Otranto,* p. xix.

[59] Platzner, ' "Gothic Versus Romantic": A Rejoinder', 267.

[60] See C. F. McIntyre, 'Were the "Gothic Novels" Gothic?', *PMLA* xxxvi (1921), 644–67, and 'The Later Career of the Elizabethan Villain-Hero', *PMLA* xl (1925), 874–80.

modal 'slippage'. This pattern is, in fact, so prevalent in the Gothic that it might be said to constitute one of its distinguishing characteristics. Repeatedly in these works, one generic mode gives way to another, leaving the reader in a state of perplexity about the author's intent. *Manfroné,* for example, carries especially crude instances of friction between the narrative of sentiment and that of adventure. One such passage struggles to unite the two modes in a meeting between the lovers Montalto and Rosalina. Rosalina has just remarked to Montalto upon the mysterious conduct of the cowled monk: '"If I mistake not signora,"' says Montalto, '"I have seen that mysterious form before, and under circumstances which make me anxious to know whether it really is one of the fathers, or a spirit that has some time attended my steps, and embittered the dearest hope which my bosom had dared to entertain." Thus having said, he cast his eyes on Rosalina, and deeply sighing, darted after the monk.'[61] *Manfroné* is replete with passages of clichéd descriptions that accord but ill with the scenes of violence that surround them:

> The beauty of the evening—the sweet tranquillity of nature—the crimson tints of departing day, fast sinking into the meditative gloom of twilight—the gentle cooling zephyr—the last soft twittering of the feathered race, as extending their wings over their downy nests, they protected their young from the damp mists of approaching night—the pale nocturnal regent . . . all served, in some measure, to lull the sorrows of Rosalina.[62]

Shortly after this meditative passage, Rosalina is gagged with a handkerchief and hurried off by Manfroné and his minions.

In later Gothic works especially, such as those of Maturin, Lewis, and Beckford, it is usual to encounter passages of self-satire, which undercut the serious tone of the narratives. In *The Milesian Chief,* Maturin delivers a lengthy spoof on sensibility in describing the behaviour of his heroine Armida,[63] and Beckford's interest in satirizing the Gothic mode is evident not only in *Vathek* but in *Azemia* and *Modern Novel Writing,* which contain sustained passages of anti-Gothic writing.

[61] *Manfroné,* i. 42–3.

[62] Ibid., i. 167.

[63] *Milesian Chief,* i. 74.

Lewis, too, wrote a burlesque of the sentimental school of fiction before he composed *The Monk.* As early as *The Castle of Otranto,* it is often difficult to determine whether the author is engaging in 'straight Gothic' or burlesque, as conventional Gothic depends so heavily on exaggeration to convey moods of intensity and scenes of action. Walpole's comment to Élie de Beaumont about his *Castle of Otranto* suggests his awareness of the tendency of Gothic to teeter on the brink of tragedy and comedy, between the sublime and the ridiculous: 'If I make you laugh, for I cannot flatter myself that I shall make you cry,' he wrote, 'I shall be content . . . '[64] The remark is not merely the self-protective gesture of the uncertain novelist; it reveals Walpole's awareness of the strong comic elements in his own work, elements that are present in most examples of the genre.[65] Byron's *Manfred,* interestingly, perhaps in response to this Gothic tendency to relieve intensity by low comedy, originally included a slapstick scene in which Ashtaroth carried off the Abbot. It was removed at the advice of William Gifford.

Stage adaptations of Gothic novels, interestingly, tended to emphasize these comic elements over and above the terrific ones, purging—or, more often, perverting into comedy—the main horrors of the original piece.[66] This tendency to utilize the supernatural as the focus of comedy rather than terror is evident in an opera inspired in part by Radcliffe's *Sicilian Romance* and *The Mysteries of Udolpho:* Miles Peter Andrews's *Mysteries of the Castle.* The play opens with the arrival at Messina of Carlos, who has come from Savoy to avenge the supposed death of his lover Julia. In the second act, Carlos and his effete friend Hilario enter an old room of a castle hung with tattered tapestry. The stage is darkened, and thunder and lightning flash through the old walls. Despite the fact that they expect to find Julia's remains in the castle vault, Hilario's

[64] Walpole to Jean-Baptiste-Jacques Élie de Beaumont, 18 Mar. 1765, *Correspondence*, xl. 380.

[65] Compare, for example, the exclamations of Paulo at the end of *The Italian* and the figures of Leonella and Jacintha in *The Monk.*

[66] See W. Thorp, 'The Stage Adventures of Some Gothic Novels', *PMLA* xliii (1928), 476–86; B. Evans, *Gothic Drama from Walpole to Shelley,* University of California Publications in English, xviii (Berkeley and Los Angeles, 1947).

remarks throughout the scene generate humour rather than fear:

CARLOS. Mark me—observe that window—do you not see a light? (*a light is seen to pass*)

HILARIO. A Li—ght!

CARLOS. It points me out the way—brightens, and animates the darken'd scene. . . . Heaven is in our cause—something is to be done, haste—follow. [*Runs out thro' one of the doors in the Scene.*

HILARIO (*alone*) Follow! I'm numb'd, I'm petrified—I have not a limb to stand upon—soft—let me try (*advances one leg*) yes, I have put my right foot foremost, no, let me take it back again. *(retreats a little)* [*Thunders again*

What shall I leave my friend in the lurch? let him grapple with old Ebony by himself? for shame, Hilario! after him, my boy!

[*Goes towards the doors in the Scene, opens one on the right of that where Carlos entered, which discovers a Coffin standing on a bier, with a lamp upon it.*

Wheugh! I'm dead and buried! a Coffin! (*shuts door*) and I dare say the sexton will be here before I can say my pray'rs . . .[67]

Thorp's explanation of this tendency to emphasize the comic elements of the supernatural is that the public was 'not yet willing to suffer a romanticized theater';[68] another interpretative possibility is that the playwrights were elaborating on the self-satiric strain that was a strong mark of many of the Gothic romances upon which they based their work. This 'structurally miscellaneous' or tonally disjunctive quality of the Gothic is one of the genre's most significant and overlooked features. In this regard, it displays congruities with Gothic architecture that are striking. John Evelyn's description of Gothic structures in his 'Account of Architects and Architecture' of 1697 is representative of later assessments of eighteenth-century Gothic literature:

It was after the Irruption, and Swarmes of those Truculent People from the *North;* the *Moors* and *Arabs* from the *South* and *East,* over-running the Civiliz'd World; that wherever they fix'd themselves, they soon began to Debauch this Noble and Useful Art [of the *Ancients*]; when instead of those Beautiful *Orders,* so Majestical and

[67] Miles Peter Andrews, *The Mysteries of the Castle: A Dramatic Tale, in Three Acts* (London, 1795), II. i, pp. 38–9.

[68] Thorp, 'Stage Adventures', 476.

Proper for their Stations, becoming Variety, and other Ornamental Accessories; they set up those Slender and Misquine *Pillars*, or rather bundles of *Staves*, and other incongruous Props, to support incumbent Weights, and pondrous Arched Roofs, without *Entablature;* and tho' not without great Industry (as *M. D'Aviler* well observes) nor altogether Naked of Gaudy *Sculpture*, trite and busy Carvings; 'tis such as rather Gluts the Eye, than Gratifies and Pleases it with any reasonable Satisfaction: For Proof of this, [let] any Man of Judgment [gaze] a while upon *King Henry* the VIIth's *Chappel* at *Westminster* . . . on its sharp *Angles, Jetties,* Narrow Lights, lame *Statues, Lace* and other *Cut-work* and *Crinkle Crankle;* and . . . then turn his Eyes on the *Banqueting-House* built at *White-Hall* by *Inego Jones* after the Antient manner . . . the Universal and unreasonable Thickness of the Walls, Clumsy Buttresses, Towers, sharp pointed Arches, Doors, and other Apertures, without Proportion; Non-Sense Insertions of various Marbles impertinently plac'd; Turrets, and Pinacles thick set with *Munkies* and *Chimaeras* (and abundance of buisy Work and other Incongruities) dissipate, and break the Angels [*sic*] of the Sight, and so Confound it, that one cannot consider it with any Steadiness, where to begin or end; taking off from that Noble *Aier* and *Grandure*, Bold and Graceful manner, which the Antients had so well, and judiciously Established . . .[69]

Evelyn's description of the disproportions and gaudy decorations of Gothic architecture might serve equally well as an account of the peculiar structure of Gothic narratives. The experience of confusion, of disjunction—whether tonal, modal, or structural—is central to many Gothic novels. On most occasions, these disjunctive or disturbing effects are controlled by the authors—as when Lewis increases the speed of his narration in the carriage ride of Raymond and the Bleeding Nun in *The Monk*, or when Walpole interrupts his narrative by death throes or unexpected events in *The Castle of Otranto*. Of more importance than these rather simple devices of causing unease in the reader are moments in which the disjunctions are inadvertent or farther reaching. Wylie Sypher, for example, has argued in a searching analysis of *The Mysteries of Udolpho*

[69] John Evelyn, 'An Account of Architects and Architecture . . .', in R. Fréart, *A Parallel of the Antient Architecture with the Modern*, 2nd edn. (London, 1707), pp. 9–10. Parallels between Gothic literature and art have been discussed since the genre's inception. For a recent treatment see Bayer-Berenbaum, *The Gothic Imagination*.

that the tonal and modal disjunctiveness in the romances of Radcliffe betrays an unresolved conflict between an essentially bourgeois and a radical or romantic point of view: *The Mysteries of Udolpho,* he concludes, 'is morally directed toward caution . . . and a proper restraint of generosity while it is aesthetically directed toward an indulgence of sentiment to the degree of incaution'.[70] Thus, it is a novel that is 'unintentionally subversive, unwittingly ambiguous'.[71] Radcliffe's Gothic, for Sypher, is thus not socially revolutionary. In failing to resolve its moral and aesthetic values, it falls uncomfortably between the revolutionary and the conservative, successful only at failing to be entirely either. Such stylistic disjunctions are, as I have attempted to show, hallmarks of Gothic narrative: rent by conflicting intentions, attracted to the disparities it creates, it straddles—usually unsuccessfully, because it fails to confront the significance of its own position—two essentially juxtaposed ways of narrating and characterizing.

[70] 'Social Ambiguity in a Gothic Novel', *Partisan Review,* xii (1945), 54.
[71] Ibid., 53.

3 Frenzy: *The Castle of Otranto*

> People of constant curiosity have no particular object in view: their minds being totally vacant, they want something new to fill every moment: but having no suite in their ideas, the next moment is as empty as the former and wants equally to be replenished. They are like young birds in a nest, that gape and gobble, and gape again.
>
> Memorandum in Walpole's hand, 'Autograph Diary of Admission to Strawberry Hill, 1784–1796'

'He loved mischief', Macaulay wrote of Horace Walpole: 'but he loved quiet; and he was constantly on the watch for opportunities of gratifying both his tastes at once.'[1] Walpole's turbulent attitude to the 'serious' world has been remarked upon by all his biographers—cultivating an air of detachment ('Never mind the town and its filthy politics', he wrote to Montagu on 11 January 1764; 'we can go to the gallery at Strawberry . . .'),[2] he kept in constant touch with political affairs, writing pamphlets and advising others on their movements. 'Give the ministers no respite', he wrote to the Duke of Richmond. 'Press them with questions and motions . . . Call for papers . . . Talk of their waste . . .'[3] He retreated, sick of London, to his house at Twickenham, and then printed tickets and rules so that visitors could see it. 'Je ne sais en vérité plus quel homme vous êtes', Madame du Deffand wrote to Walpole in 1768; 'le panégyriste de *Richard III,* et l'auteur du *Château d'Otrante,* doit être un être bien singulier: des rêves, ou des paradoxes historiques, voilà donc à quoi vous allez employer votre loisir . . .'[4] In speaking of *The Castle of Otranto* to his

[1] Thomas Babington Macaulay, Review of *Letters of Horace Walpole . . . to Sir Horace Mann,* in the *Edinburgh Review,* lviii (1833), 228.

[2] Walpole to George Montagu, 11 Jan. 1764, *Correspondence,* x. 118.

[3] Walpole to the Duke of Richmond, 27 Oct. 1775, *Correspondence,* xli. 310–11.

[4] Madame du Deffand to Walpole, 12 Jan. 1768, *Correspondence,* iv. 6.

friends, Walpole liked to emphasize this double-sidedness, boasting of his connection to a world of public responsibility while pretending to eschew all association with it. To both Montagu and Cole he wrote that the book was conceived 'in the midst of grave nonsense and foolish councils of war'.[5] 'The work grew on my hands', he told Cole, 'and I grew fond of it—add that I was very glad to think of anything rather than politics . . .'[6]

That *The Castle of Otranto* was composed at a time of political turmoil became a source of particular interest to Walpole, who treated it frequently as a sign of his wilful retreat from the exigencies of the real world: 'We are extremely amused', he wrote to Hertford of a wolf that had killed a number of peasants in Languedoc, 'with the wonderful histories of your hyena in the Gévaudan . . . it is exactly the enchanted monster of old romances. If I had known its history a few months ago, I believe it would have appeared in the *Castle of Otranto* . . .'[7] The intimate association of *The Castle of Otranto* and Strawberry Hill[8] and Walpole's tendency to use both as symbols of romantic escape suggest that the novel (like Strawberry Hill) may serve as a locus for an intentional and privileged shuffling off of responsibilities of all kinds. Walpole expected that Cole would think him 'idle' in devoting time to his romance,[9] and *The Castle of Otranto* (through its connection with Strawberry Hill), indeed becomes linked with some of the same qualities of deliberate quaintness as Walpole's villa and some of the same boyish lapses of taste and defiant

[5] Walpole to George Montagu, 26 May 1765, *Correspondence,* x. 154.

[6] Walpole to the Revd William Cole, 9 Mar. 1765, *Correspondence,* i. 88.

[7] Walpole to Hertford, 26 Mar. 1765, *Correspondence,* xxxviii. 525.

[8] Walpole spoke frequently of the influence of Strawberry Hill on *The Castle of Otranto,* and by 1784 had announced the connection publicly, describing his house as 'a very proper habitation of, as it was the scene that inspired, the author of the Castle of Otranto' (*A Description of the Villa of Mr. Horace Walpole . . . at Strawberry-Hill near Twickenham* . . . (Strawberry Hill, 1784), p. iv). W. S. Lewis and Warren Hunting Smith, taking Walpole's reference to a 'certain building' in the first preface to *The Castle of Otranto* to mean Strawberry Hill, have pointed out the similarities between Otranto and Strawberry Hill (as well as between Otranto and Trinity College, Cambridge). See W. S. Lewis, 'The Genesis of Strawberry Hill', *Metropolitan Museum Studies,* v. i (1934), 88–90; W. H. Smith, 'Strawberry Hill and Otranto', *TLS* 23 May 1936, p. 440.

[9] Walpole to the Revd William Cole, 9 Mar. 1765, *Correspondence,* i. 88.

disregard for protocol. Like Strawberry Hill, *The Castle of Otranto* was created primarily 'to realize [Walpole's] own visions',[10] as a *jeu d'esprit* magnifying, comically, some of the eccentricities of his own that he found most charming. This self-reflective quality of Walpole's tale is its most distinctive feature, and the aspect of the story that has been most resistant to critical commentary. Throughout *The Castle of Otranto*, Walpole's delight in indulging his taste for medievalism and his fascination with the irresponsibility of this activity give rise to peculiar tonal and modal discordances that produce, as early as the first preface, an atmosphere of disorder and confusion that permeates both the tale's style and its intent.

DEFINING OTRANTO

The discords and evasions that characterize *The Castle of Otranto* are enunciated in the theoretical discussions in Walpole's second preface to his novel. Challenged (after he decides to reveal his authorship) to provide a justification of his tale, Walpole is unable to arrive at a coherent one, yet by repeatedly insisting on the unorthodox qualities of the work he convinces himself that he has embarked on something genuinely new. In seeking to define that newness, however, he falls back on old definitions of romance and the serio-comic and, calling forth the precedent of Shakespeare, he shifts his focus away from his own work into a lengthy criticism of Voltaire, an area in which he feels on sounder theoretical footing. Interestingly, in the preface to the first edition, Walpole (as translator) felt no need to provide such commentary: the tale is presented, rather, as a curiosity defensible in its own right, an artefact from 'the darkest ages of Christianity', the days of 'ancient errors and superstitions', whose most striking aspect is its ghosts and whose present function is entertainment:

> Whatever [the author's] views were, or whatever effects the execution of them might have, his work can only be laid before the public at present as a matter of entertainment. Even as such, some apology for it is necessary. Miracles, visions, necromancy, dreams, and other

[10] Walpole, *Description of ... Strawberry-Hill*, p. iv.

preternatural events, are exploded now even from romances. That was not the case when our author wrote; much less when the story itself is supposed to have happened. Belief in every kind of prodigy was so established in those dark ages, that an author would not be faithful to the *manners* of the times who should omit all mention of them. He is not bound to believe them himself, but he must represent his actors as believing them.[11]

In attempting to generate other, more acceptable, kinds of criteria for his novel, Walpole (though he later insisted to friends that he wrote the tale against all rule) tests the work, feebly, against the familiar conventions of the dramatic unities and the moralistic aims of romance. He praises the piece for its compactness and unity, the consistency of its characters, and the author's ability to evoke the emotions of pity and terror:

Every thing tends directly to the catastrophe. . . . The rules of the drama are almost observed throughout the conduct of the piece. The characters are well drawn, and still better maintained. Terror, the author's principal engine, prevents the story from ever languishing; and it is so often contrasted by pity, that the mind is kept up in a constant vicissitude of interesting passions.[12]

Walpole maintains, moreover, that the work is ethical in its intent: 'The piety that reigns throughout, the lessons of virtue that are inculcated, and the rigid purity of the sentiments, exempt this work from the censure to which romances are but too liable.'[13] The exaggerated gravity with which this pronouncement is made and the reductive analysis of the author's moral—*'the sins of fathers are visited on their children to the third and fourth generation'* (a moral the translator complains is not 'useful')[14]—alert the reader not only to the infirmity of Walpole's theorizing but to problems of tone that permeate the two prefaces, the work itself, and Walpole's attitude towards it. It is true, as Leigh Ehlers has recently demonstrated, that *The Castle of Otranto* is 'a Gothic *theatrum mundi* in which the hand of God operates in and through the supernatural and the human responses to such ghosts';[15] that providential interpreta-

[11] Walpole, *The Castle of Otranto: A Gothic Story,* ed. W. S. Lewis (London, 1969), p. 4. [12] Ibid., 4. [13] Ibid., 5.

[14] Ibid., 5.

[15] L. A. Ehlers, 'The Gothic World as Stage: Providence and Character in *The Castle of Otranto*', *Wascana Review*, xiv. ii (1979), 18.

tions for events are repeatedly given by Jerome and Hippolita; that Manfred, abusing power, is punished for his misdeeds; and that normal systems of hierarchy are re-established at the novel's end. To agree, however, with Walpole's assertion in the first preface that the true centre of the work lies in this retributive scheme is to overlook his delighted emphasis on discord and incongruity, and his violation and exaggeration of the very rules he maintains dictated the composition of the piece. Walpole's veering in both prefaces from an apparently serious to an obviously ironic tone alerts the reader to the importance of the question of Walpole's attitude towards the work—a question that Walpole repeatedly brings up in correspondence to his friends about his story. His petulant insistence to Madame du Deffand that he wrote the work in despite of rules, heated by his own passions and visions, provides, perhaps, the most accurate assessment of his motivations.[16] *The Castle of Otranto,* thus, becomes the ultimate kind of escape: liberated by visions, Walpole yet insists that he is tying it down by rules. Vowing in the second preface that he has 'created a new species of romance', he evades defining that newness (perhaps because he is reluctant to confront what that novelty consists of or because he has not yet developed the terminology with which to speak of it) by suggesting that he took his cues from Shakespeare. The paragraph that closes the second preface is a masterpiece of critical hedging: Walpole, who has already allowed his analysis of his romance to be interrupted by a consideration of Voltaire's response to Shakespeare, follows the same pattern of posing the work as original and then refusing to take full responsibility for it:

The result of all I have said is to shelter my own daring under the cannon of the brightest genius this country, at least, has produced. I might have pleaded, that having created a new species of romance, I was at liberty to lay down what rules I thought fit for the conduct of it: but I should be more proud of having imitated, however faintly, weakly, and at a distance, so masterly a pattern, than to enjoy the entire merit of invention, unless I could have marked my work with genius as well as with originality. Such as it is, the public have honoured it sufficiently, whatever rank their suffrages allot to it.[17]

[16] Walpole to Madame du Deffand, 13 Mar. 1767, no. 55, *Correspondence*, iii. 260.

[17] *The Castle of Otranto,* p. 12.

It is clear at last that there are no rules for the conduct of this new species of romance, that Walpole's 'daring', 'invention', and 'originality' are as yet qualities of composition that he will name but that he will not, for some reason, analyse. Instead, he retreats into fumbling: 'Such as it is [what *is* it?], the public have honoured it sufficiently . . .'[18] It is, finally, impossible to accept Walpole's sober explanation of his motivations for the work's creation— 'It was an attempt', he says, 'to blend the two kinds of romance, the ancient and the modern'[19]—in part because of the hasty retreat he beats from his own theorizing (escaping from the consideration of his own story into the familiar territory of Shakespeare and Voltaire) and in part because of the odd mistakes he makes about the tone of his work.

TONE

Even in the first preface, Walpole startles the reader by asserting that there is 'no bombast' in his work. Part of the comedy of *The Castle of Otranto* (and it is obvious, from an examination of the work and of Walpole's descriptions of it to his friends, that the work is essentially comic in character) lies in Manfred's bombast: 'Lead on!' he cries to the dejected spectre who steps from the picture frame. 'I will follow thee to the gulph of perdition.'[20] Walpole's repeated descriptions of the work as 'solemn', 'tragic', and 'moving'[21]—he calls his heroes' passions 'grave', 'important', 'melancholy', and even 'sublime'—and his association of *The Castle of Otranto* with *Hamlet* and *Julius Caesar* (and, later, with 'inspired writings')[22] suggest a misapprehension about the tone of the work that would be almost unthinkable for an author as well versed as he was in the art of parody.[23] It is nearly impossible, in fact, to reconcile this insistence on the work's theoretical and tonal seriousness in the

[18] Ibid., 12. [19] Ibid., 7. [20] Ibid., 24. [21] Ibid., 9; 10; 6.

[22] Ibid., 8.

[23] Walpole's remarks to Bertie Greatheed about his son's drawings for *The Castle of Otranto,* however, seem to challenge this view: 'I have seen many drawings and prints made from my idle—I don't know what to call it, novel or romance—not one of them approached to any one of your son's four—a clear proof of which is, that not one of the rest satisfied the author's ideas.—It is as strictly, and upon my honour, true, that your son's conception of some of the passions has improved them, and added more expres-

preface with Walpole's emphasis in his letters to friends on the tale's 'quaintness' and on its comedy. 'I have received C. of O.', Gray wrote to Walpole on 30 December 1764, 'and return you my thanks for it. It engages our attention here, makes some of us cry a little, and all in general afraid to go to bed o'nights. We take it for a translation, and should believe it to be a true story, if it were not for St Nicholas'.[24] Gray had, by the time of this letter, already read the manuscript for *The Castle of Otranto* and encouraged Walpole to publish it, so his judgement of the tale is likely to confirm an attitude that he had already taken towards the work and one that Walpole had found agreeable.

What is striking about Gray's letter is the tongue-in-cheek tone he adopts in it towards Walpole's novel, treating it not as a serious piece but as one that plays in a frivolous, satirical way with its readers' emotions: 'it engages our attention here, makes *some of us* cry *a little,* and all *in general* afraid to go to bed o'nights.' In adopting the overly sober attitude of Swift's Bishop (who rejected *Gulliver's Travels* as 'full of improbable lies'), Gray hints at the whimsical qualities of the work, as well as at Walpole's intention of 'duping' his audience (an attribute of the work that Walpole, especially when the tale met with criticism, fell back on with pleasure). Such a stance provides Walpole with a guaranteed escape route: if the tale fails to amuse, it is only a joke anyway; if the audience falls for it, one ostensible purpose of the work has been fulfilled. 'J'ai voulu qu'elle passât pour ancienne', Walpole wrote to Madame du Deffand, 'et presque tout le monde en fut la dupe.'[25]

Amidst these deliberate confusions of tone and intent, one facet of the work is presented consistently by Walpole, and that is the connection of his novel to the imagination (as opposed to

sion than I myself had formed in my own mind; for example, in the figure of the ghost in the chapel, to whose hollow sockets your son has given an air of reproachful anger, and to the whole turn of his person, dignity. Manfred in the last scene has an uncertain horror, that shows he has not yet had time to know what kind of agony he feels at what he has done. Such delineation of passions at so very youthful a period, or rather in boyhood, are indubitable indications of real genius . . .' (*Correspondence,* xlii. 430). Whether Walpole is serious here or merely attempting to flatter (or even dupe) Greatheed is difficult to determine.

[24] Thomas Gray to Walpole, 30 Dec. 1764, *Correspondence,* xiv. 137.

[25] Walpole to Madame du Deffand, 13 Mar. 1767, no. 55, *Correspondence*, iii. 261.

'cold reason'). In the first preface, Walpole accounts for this quality of the piece by the superstitious attitudes of the work's 'original' readers, by their interest in necromancy and visions which the present age has exploded. In the second preface, he brings the issue up to date, complaining of the 'great resources of fancy' which in modern romance 'have been dammed up, by a strict adherence to common life'.[26] In linking writing with the release of the imagination ('leaving the powers of fancy at liberty to expatiate through the boundless realms of invention')[27] and in trying to speak responsibly of what he has done, it becomes apparent that Walpole associates imaginative activity with incongruity and discords of all kinds, discords that penetrate not only his work, but the way he talks about his work to others. The difficulties critics have had in agreeing on the tone of *The Castle of Otranto* evidence the complexity of Walpole's presentation of his novel. It has become commonplace to speak of *The Castle of Otranto* as 'a castle of horrors',[28] yet Walpole repeatedly referred to his tale as 'amusing', as a 'trifle' and a 'plaisanterie'. '[I]f I have amused you', he wrote to Cole on 9 March 1765, 'by retracing with any fidelity the manners of ancient days, I am content, and give you leave to think me as idle as you please'.[29] His dedication to Lady Mary Coke encouraged her not to tremble but to 'smile' at the work. Walpole's pointed refusal to speak of his novel as serious or horrifying may, of course, be the defensive posture of an author reluctant to subject himself to criticism, yet his attitude towards his tragedy, *The Mysterious Mother,* suggests that he was willing to admit openly to a 'serious' piece of his own when he saw it. He realized very quickly that his drama would be too horrifying to stage and he guarded the work's circulation with extreme care. Walpole's deliberate thwarting of a unified response to *The Castle of Otranto* has produced a marked ambivalence in the critics' reactions to the novel: Scott, who calls the work in one breath 'a tale of amusing fiction', 'one of the standard works of our lighter literature', also treats it seriously, saying that it contains scenes of grandeur and excites the pas-

[26] *The Castle of Otranto,* p. 7.

[27] Ibid., 7.

[28] See, for example, M. M. Tatar, 'The Houses of Fiction: Toward a Definition of the Uncanny', *Comparative Literature,* xxxiii (1981), 171.

[29] Walpole to the Revd William Cole, 9 Mar. 1765, *Correspondence,* i. 88.

sions of fear and pity.[30] Stanley Solomon is persuaded that the novel is deliberately ironic,[31] and Leslie Stephen that it 'passes the borders of the burlesque'.[32] This division of opinions (a characteristic of criticism of the Gothic from the genre's inception) is perhaps the most truthful response to Walpole's chaotic tale: destabilized by contradictions in tone, then energized by what would become two of the most favoured of Gothic techniques—rapid pace and escalation—the work exhibits a systematic disregard for unities that Walpole clearly relates to personal and imaginative art.

The tonal and modal discordances in *The Castle of Otranto* are among the tale's most striking stylistic features (as they tend to be, indeed, in much Gothic narrative) and the sources of most of the work's comedy. Walpole's interest in the novel's humorous moments is clear; he defends the use of comedy in both prefaces, and often extends his comic scenes to ridiculous lengths, building suspense through capricious delays of the main action. The fact that Walpole in his prefatorial treatments of this technique discusses these scenes primarily to stress the 'serious' cast of his work hints at the possibility of burlesque; the laughable emotions of the servants, he says, serve to heighten the pathetic impact of the main characters:

> The simplicity of their behaviour, almost tending to excite smiles, which at first seem not consonant to the serious cast of the work, appeared to me not only not improper, but was marked designedly in that manner. My rule was nature. However grave, important, or even melancholy, the sensations of princes and heroes may be, they do not stamp the same affections on their domestics: at least the latter do not, or should not be made to express their passions in the same dignified tone. In my humble opinion, the contrast between the sublime of the one, and the *naïveté* of the other, sets the pathetic of the former in a stronger light.[33]

The gravity with which these dicta are uttered and the final tribute to Shakespeare in which he implicitly compares *The Castle of Otranto* to *Hamlet* and *Julius Caesar* raise three

[30] [Sir Walter Scott], in his introd. to *The Castle of Otranto; A Gothic Story* (Edinburgh, 1811), pp. iii; xvi; xxxvi.

[31] S. J. Solomon, 'Subverting Propriety as a Pattern of Irony in Three Eighteenth-century Novels: *The Castle of Otranto, Vathek,* and *Fanny Hill*', *Erasmus Review,* i (1971), 107–16.

[32] L. Stephen, 'Horace Walpole', in *Hours in a Library,* new edn., with additions (4 vols., London, 1907), ii. 138.

[33] *The Castle of Otranto,* p. 8.

possibilities: either Walpole seriously believes that he has rendered *The Castle of Otranto* in as Shakespearian a manner as possible; or, recognizing the shaky foundation on which he has tried to construct a defence of his novel, is turning his attention to a more congenial topic; or he is engaging in an intentional burlesque. Walpole's interest in Shakespeare's use of comedy is clear from many remarks in his essays and letters; he thought of it as one of Shakespeare's foremost gifts. But a cursory examination of the comic scenes in Walpole's novel suggests that they do not function to 'set the pathetic of [his heroes] in a stronger light',[34] nor do they elicit serious remarks—two of the main functions of the comic as Walpole defined it later in a note on Garrick's production of *Hamlet* in 1773:

In 1773. Mr Garrick produced his Hamlet altered, in which he had omitted the scene of the grave diggers, from injudicious complaisance to French critics, and their cold regularity, which cramps genius. Objections made to that admirable scene of nature, is, that it is burlesque, unheroic, and destroys and interrupts the interest of the action, and diverts Hamlet from his purpose on which he ought only to think, the vengeance due to the murder of his father. Not one of these objections are true. If Garrick had really been an intelligent manager, he would have corrected the vicious buffoonery which lay in his actors, not in the play. The parts of the grave-diggers have long been played by the most comic and buffoon actors in the company, who always endeavoured to raise a laughter from the galleries by absurd mirth and gesticulations. The parts ought to be given [to them] who could best represent low nature seriously, and at most the jokes between the men themselves previous to Hamlet's entry might have been shortened, tho those very jests are natural and moral, for they show that habit can bring men to be cheerful even in the midst of the most melancholy exercise of their profession. That the scene is not unheroic, tho in prose, is from the serious remarks it draws from Hamlet. Is every low character inconsistent with heroic tragedy? What has so pathetic effect as the fool in Lear?[35]

Walpole's comic scenes not only lack pathetic effect; they consistently function to cast ridicule on Walpole's villain

[34] Ibid., 8.

[35] Horace Walpole, *Notes by Horace Walpole on Several Characters of Shakespeare*, ed. W. S. Lewis, Miscellaneous Antiquities, xvi (Farmington, Conn., 1940), pp. 5–6.

Manfred, rendering him a victim of his servants' incompetence —laughable and powerless, not tragic. Repeatedly, Manfred's domestics step in (or out) at inopportune times, officiously revealing information Manfred has sought to keep hidden or insisting with stupid persistence on a fact that immediately reveals Manfred's dark designs. Manfred's inability to control himself in such scenes heightens their ridiculous impact. The 'Marx Brothers' style rendition by Diego and Jaquez of their view of the ghost's foot and part of his leg goes on for three and a half pages, while Manfred loses all control over himself and the situation:

While the prince was in this suspense, a confused noise of voices echoed through the distant vaults. As the sound approached, he distinguished the clamour of some of his domestics, whom he had dispersed through the castle in search of Isabella, calling out, Where is my lord? Where is the prince? Here I am, said Manfred, as they came nearer; have you found the princess? The first that arrived replied, Oh, my lord! I am glad we have found you.—Found me! said Manfred: have you found the princess? We thought we had, my lord, said the fellow looking terrified—but—But what? cried the prince: has she escaped?—Jaquez and I, my lord—Yes, I and Diego, interrupted the second, who came up in still greater consternation—Speak one of you at a time, said Manfred; I ask you, where is the princess? We do not know, said they both together: but we are frightened out of our wits.— So I think, blockheads, said Manfred: what is it has scared you thus?—Oh, my lord! said Jaquez, Diego has seen such a sight! your highness would not belief our eyes.—What new absurdity is this? cried Manfred—Give me a direct answer, or by heaven—Why, my lord, if it please your highness to hear me, said the poor fellow; Diego and I—Yes, I and Jaquez, cried his comrade—Did not I forbid you to speak both at a time? said the prince: You, Jaquez, answer; for the other fool seems more distracted than thou art; what is the matter? My gracious lord, said Jaquez, if it please your highness to hear me; Diego and I, according to your highness's orders, went to search for the young lady; but being comprehensive that we might meet the ghost of my young lord, your highness's son, God rest his soul, as he has not received christian burial—Sot! cried Manfred in a rage, is it only a ghost then that thou hast seen? Oh, worse! worse! my lord! cried Diego: I had rather have seen ten whole ghosts.—Grant me patience! said Manfred; these blockheads distract me—. . . .[36]

[36] *The Castle of Otranto,* pp. 30–1.

Two similarly extended scenes occur between Manfred and Bianca—first as Manfred tries to bribe Bianca to reveal what she knows about Isabella's affections, and second as he struggles to keep her from revealing his bribe in front of Frederic. In both instances, Manfred becomes an impotent, ridiculous figure, unable to command his servants or himself. Frederic questions Bianca about the hand she has seen on the banister of the great stairs:

Tell us, fair maiden [he says], what it is has moved thee thus. Yes, my lord, thank your greatness, said Bianca—I believe I look very pale; I shall be better when I have recovered myself.—I was going to my lady Isabella's chamber by his highness's order—We do not want the circumstances, interrupted Manfred: since his highness will have it so, proceed; but be brief.—Lord, your highness thwarts one so! replied Bianca—I fear my hair—I am sure I never in my life—Well! as I was telling your greatness, I was going by his highness's order to my lady Isabella's chamber: she lies in the watchet-coloured chamber, on the right hand, one pair of stairs: so when I came to the great stairs—I was looking on his highness's present here. Grant me patience! said Manfred, will this wench never come to the point? What imports it to the marquis, that I gave thee a bawble for thy faithful attendance on my daughter? We want to know what thou sawest. I was going to tell your highness, said Bianca, if you would permit me.—So, as I was rubbing the ring—I am sure I had not gone up three steps, but I heard the rattling of armour; for all the world such a clatter, as Diego says he heard when the giant turned him about in the gallery-chamber.—What does she mean, my lord? said the marquis. Is your castle haunted by giants and goblins?—Lord, what, has not your greatness heard the story of the giant in the gallery-chamber? cried Bianca. I marvel his highness has not told you—mayhap you do not know there is a prophecy—This trifling is intolerable, interrupted Manfred. Let us dismiss this silly wench, my lord: we have more important affairs to discuss.[37]

That such scenes advance the plot is indisputable; in a tale based on hidden identities and the fulfilment of mysterious prophecies, any revelation of the true disposition of characters and things will function to move the story forward to its catastrophe. But it would be ridiculous to contend that they function in a way similar to the gravediggers' scene in *Hamlet,* for, instead of creating two levels of response, they work in a bathetic way to sink all into comedy. The references to

[37] Ibid., 99.

Shakespeare in the preface to *The Castle of Otranto* are themselves certainly not ironic; but Walpole had enough critical judgement to know that his scenes were in no way Shakespearian.

THE SENTIMENTAL AND THE BURLESQUE

The friction produced by this jettisoning of the tragic by the comic has its counterpart in another modal incongruity that would become a central feature of later Gothic tales: the reversion to the situations and vocabulary of sentimental romance. Walpole's dedication to Lady Mary Coke emphasizes such facets of his story and encourages a sentimental response:

> The gentle maid, whose hapless tale
> These melancholy pages speak;
> Say, gracious lady, shall she fail
> To draw the tear adown thy cheek?
> No; never was thy pitying breast
> Insensible to human woes;
> Tender, though firm, it melts distrest
> For weaknesses it never knows.[38]

The love-encounters between Theodore and Matilda, the episode of Jerome's discovery of his son, and the scene of Matilda's death display all the conventional features of the novel of sensibility. When Matilda steals up to the black tower to release Theodore, he addresses her in the familiar tones of romance: 'Thou art surely one of those angels! said the enraptured Theodore: none but a blessed saint could speak, could act, could look like thee!—May I not know the name of my divine protectress?'[39] Theodore pleads with Matilda to let him 'bathe [her hand] with the warm tears of gratitude'[40] and, at the end of the interview, he throws himself at her feet and, 'seizing her lily hand, which with struggles she suffered him to kiss, he vowed on the earliest opportunity to get himself knighted, and fervently entreated her permission to swear himself eternally her knight'.[41] But even this passage, like a prior one depicting a conversation between Matilda and Theodore the preceding evening, is handled in such a way that a 'pure' response is forestalled. In the earlier scene, in which Matilda becomes romantically interested in Theodore, Bianca's

[38] Ibid., 13. [39] Ibid., 68–9. [40] Ibid., 69. [41] Ibid., 71.

pragmatic remarks ('Do, madam, let us sift him') and malapropisms ('it is very particular though, that my lady Isabella should be missing on the same day') puncture the mood of romantic mystery, and the degeneration of the conversation into Bianca's humorous attempts to prove that Isabella is a hypocrite makes the scene as much a spoof on the sentimental interlude as the later one, in which the dialogue between Theodore and Matilda is interrupted by a groan attributed to 'pent-up vapours' and is closed by a clap of thunder that shakes the battlements.[42] Isabella's sudden concern about the propriety of disappearing into a cave with Theodore to escape the designs of the infamous Manfred sounds a similarly discordant note: 'But come, lady,' Theodore urges her, 'we are too near the mouth of the cavern; let us seek its inmost recesses: I can have no tranquillity till I have placed thee beyond the reach of danger.' '—Alas! what mean you, sir?' Isabella replies. 'Though all your actions are noble, though your sentiments speak the purity of your soul, is it fitting that I should accompany you alone into these perplexed retreats? Should we be found together, what would a censorious world think of my conduct?'[43] It is a measure of Walpole's subtlety in playing with these modes that illustrators of the novel chose repeatedly to depict the sentimental scenes of the story, giving prominence sometimes exclusively to the hero and heroines. One French translator of *The Castle of Otranto* was so taken by the sentimental strain of the narrative that he retitled the novel *Isabelle et Théodore.*[44] It is difficult (as always) to identify Walpole's true response to this facet of his work: the meeting between Theodore and Jerome is meant to evoke pathos (inasmuch as one can sympathize with characters one hardly knows) and Walpole refrains in that scene from the investigation of minute particulars that usually leads him to satire or bathos, remarking that '[t]he passions that ensued must be conceived; they cannot be painted.'[45] Later, Jerome, 'falling on the neck of his son', discharges the conventional flood of tears, 'that spoke the fulness of his soul'.[46] Both these scenes, however, lack the extended treatment of incident or character

[42] Ibid., 41; 43; 70; 71. [43] Ibid., 73.
[44] *Isabelle et Théodore* (Paris, 1797).
[45] *The Castle of Otranto*, p. 54. [46] Ibid., 57.

that could generate a true sentimental response. The account of the spat between Matilda and Isabella over Theodore, on the other hand, is rendered in more detail and introduces into the novel a note of domestic comedy that threatens to undo Walpole's sentimental tale of wonders. The scene of Matilda's death, despite (or perhaps because of) the agonized breast-beatings that precede it, is clearly burlesque in tone: '—oh!—She expired.'[47] Theodore, at the story's end, bending to the structural demand that a tale of sensibility conclude in marriage, weds Isabella in a lachrymose version of a sentimental finale: ' . . . Theodore's grief was too fresh to admit the thought of another love; and it was not till after frequent discourses with Isabella, of his dear Matilda, that he was persuaded he could know no happiness but in the society of one with whom he could forever indulge the melancholy that had taken possession of his soul'.[48]

As in the love scene between Theodore and Matilda, in which a sound like 'pent-up vapours' rudely interrupts the conversants, even the supernatural in Walpole's novel is subjected to occasional burlesque treatment. Many of Walpole's earlier critics commented on his maladroitness in handling his spectres. 'Its action and interference', Scott wrote of Walpole's ghostly machinery, 'is rather too frequent, and presses too hard and constantly upon the same feelings in the reader's mind, to the hazard of diminishing the elasticity of the spring upon which it should operate.'[49] 'The great hand and arm,' Hazlitt wrote less kindly and less accurately, 'which are thrust into the court-yard, and remain there all day long, are the pasteboard machinery of a pantomime; they shock the senses, and have no purchase upon the imagination. They are a matter-of-fact impossibility; a fixture, and no longer a phantom.'[50] Walpole, indeed, tends to overdo his supernatural effects: one portent follows another in rapid succession; plumes wave and a portrait steps from its frame in a raree-show of spectral events. The phantasmagoric scenes take on the structure of a pastiche:

[47] Ibid., 107. [48] Ibid., 110.

[49] [Scott], introd. to *The Castle of Otranto*, p. xxvii.

[50] William Hazlitt, 'Lecture VI: On the English Novelists', from *Lectures on the English Comic Writers* (1819), *The Complete Works of William Hazlitt*, ed. P. P. Howe (21 vols., London, 1930–4), vi. 127.

Manfred, distracted between the flight of Isabella, who had now reached the stairs, and his inability to keep his eyes from the picture, which began to move, had however advanced some steps after her, still looking backwards on the portrait, when he saw it quit its pannel, and descend on the floor with a grave and melancholy air. Do I dream? cried Manfred returning, or are the devils themselves in league against me? Speak, infernal spectre! Or, if thou are my grandsire, why dost thou too conspire against thy wretched descendant, who too dearly pays for—Ere he could finish the sentence the vision sighed again, and made a sign to Manfred to follow him. Lead on! cried Manfred; I will follow thee to the gulph of perdition. The spectre marched sedately, but dejected, to the end of the gallery, and turned into a chamber on the right hand. Manfred accompanied him at a little distance, full of anxiety and horror, but resolved. As he would have entered the chamber, the door was clapped-to with violence by an invisible hand. The prince, collecting courage from this delay, would have forcibly burst open the door with his foot, but found that it resisted his utmost efforts. Since hell will not satisfy my curiosity, said Manfred, I will use the human means in my power for preserving my race; Isabella shall not escape me.[51]

When, towards the end of the story, the gigantic sword bursts from its bearers and falls to the ground beside the helmet, Manfred returns quietly to the hall, 'almost hardened', as Walpole writes, 'to preternatural appearances'.[52] We take our cue from Manfred; weary of falling bodies and dismembered limbs, we shrug this one off with idle curiosity.

PACE

This tonal instability of *The Castle of Otranto* lends an air of recklessness to the novel that is intensified by the story's pace. If Walpole's critics expressed uncertainty about the efficacy of his spectres and the effect of his characters, they almost all agreed on his ability to keep the reader entertained. 'The story', in Macaulay's words, '. . . never flags for a single moment. There are no digressions, or unseasonable descriptions, or long speeches. Every sentence carries the action forward. The excitement is constantly renewed.'[53] Walpole emphasized this quality of his story-telling in the preface to the first edition:

[51] *The Castle of Otranto,* p. 24. [52] Ibid., 63.

[53] Macaulay, Review of *Letters of Horace Walpole,* 265–6.

'Never is the reader's attention relaxed. . . . Terror, the author's principal engine, prevents the story from ever languishing; and it is so often contrasted by pity, that the mind is kept up in a constant vicissitude of interesting passions.'[54]

In recounting the story of the novel's inception, Walpole liked to call attention to the extempore nature of its composition and the speed with which it was written:

I waked one morning in the beginning of last June from a dream [he wrote to Cole on 9 March 1765], of which all I could recover was, that I had thought myself in an ancient castle (a very natural dream for a head filled like mine with Gothic story) and that on the uppermost bannister of a great staircase I saw a gigantic hand in armour. In the evening I sat down and began to write, without knowing in the least what I intended to say or relate. The work grew on my hands, and I grew fond of it . . . In short I was so engrossed with my tale, which I completed in less than two months, that one evening I wrote from the time I had drunk my tea, about six o'clock, till half an hour after one in the morning, when my hand and fingers were so weary, that I could not hold the pen to finish the sentence, but left Matilda and Isabella talking, in the middle of a paragraph.[55]

Walpole repeatedly referred to his story as 'wild',[56] a 'frantic thing',[57] and liked to dwell on the details of its hasty composition, 'begun without [a] plan', as he wrote to Mason, '. . . sketched out with [no] design'.[58] For effect, he at least once telescoped the creation of the story to eight days: 'I wrote the "*Castle of Otranto*" ', he is reported to have said, 'in eight days, or rather eight nights; for my general hours of composition are from ten o'clock at night till two in the morning, when I am sure not to be disturbed by visitants. While I am writing I take several cups of coffee.'[59] Though, certainly, *The Castle of Otranto* is not as wild or spontaneous a composition as Walpole's *Hieroglyphic Tales*—stories that gave the appearance, as Walpole proudly reported, of having been written 'when I was [in the gout or] out of my senses'[60]—the pieces are

[54] *The Castle of Otranto,* p. 4.
[55] Walpole to the Revd William Cole, *Correspondence,* i. 88.
[56] Ibid., i. 88.
[57] Walpole to Hannah More, 13 Nov. 1784, *Correspondence,* xxxi. 221.
[58] Walpole to William Mason, 17 Apr. 1765, *Correspondence,* xxviii. 6.
[59] J. Pinkerton, *Walpoliana* (2 vols., London, 1799), i. 22.
[60] Walpole to the Revd William Cole, 28 Jan. 1779, *Correspondence,* ii. 142.

linked by their employment of rapid imaginative association, a quality of Walpole's prose that in *Hieroglyphic Tales* attains the uninhibited atmosphere of dreams. Surely it is the frenetic air of *The Castle of Otranto* that is its most innovative and compelling feature. Again and again, Walpole escalates the pace of his story, engaging in quick changes of scenery and interruptions that heighten our sense of the story's speed. Adaptations of *The Castle of Otranto* provide surprising evidence of the rapidity and spareness of Walpole's original narrative. One abridged version that appeared in 1765 in the *Universal Magazine* cuts the longer conversations between Isabella and Matilda and shortens the comic scenes involving the servants, leaving a tale that shows just how economical Walpole's narrative already is: large sections of the story remain virtually intact in the new version, for it contains few of the superfluous descriptions, moralizing asides, and subplots that are conventionally cropped by an abridger's shears.[61]

The pace of Walpole's tale begins to escalate immediately after the introduction of the main characters and the relation of the prophecy. One of Manfred's servants comes running out of the courtyard in speechless terror, Hippolita swoons, Manfred demands an explanation, confusion heightens, and Manfred enters the court to find his son smashed to pieces under an enormous plumed helmet. Walpole's characters 'rush', 'hasten', and 'hurry' rather than 'go'; they 'fling' and 'clap'

[61] 'The Gothic Story of the Castle of Otranto', in the *Universal Magazine*, xxxvi (1765), 202–8; 235–42. Robert Jephson's dramatic adaptation, entitled *The Count of Narbonne* (1781), indirectly reveals another facet of Walpole's narrative economy: the Manfred of the play, because he is allowed to consider his motives at some length, becomes a believable character—not, as in the original, the 'cardboard' figure of a feudal tyrant. This difference in treatment gives the reader a certain pause, for *The Castle of Otranto* seems at first to be ideally suited for the stage. Walpole alludes to this possibility several times in his first preface, calling the story a drama and utilizing the vocabulary of dramatic criticism to describe its merits. 'It is pity', he notes towards the end of his discussion, 'that [the author] did not apply his talents to what they were evidently proper for, the theatre' (p. 5). A look at Jephson's play makes apparent that *The Castle of Otranto*, paradoxically, pushes the notion of the dramatic so far that it is tolerable only in narrative. It is perhaps for this reason that relatively few of Walpole's illustrators were willing to depict the dramatic and supernatural aspects of his tale, concentrating instead on the story's more static sentimental and heraldic scenes. A striking (later) exception is the Christmas pantomime, *The Castle of Otranto; or, Harlequin and the Giant Helmet*, performed in 1840 and 1841 at Covent Garden, with gigantic props and stupendous scenery. In this adaptation, however, the work is presented as an outright burlesque.

doors to, and make sudden movements that strain the narrative and keep it moving at a pitch of excitement that is meant, one supposes, to provide a physical analogue to the experience of emotional turmoil. But, as Robert Kiely has demonstrated, this traumatization of the physical plane of the narrative has little connection with the inner life of Walpole's characters—in large part because they have no inner life that would give such gestures significance.[62] The result is a story that speeds along at a remarkable rate unencumbered by deeper meaning.

The speed and structure of Walpole's narrative point to a preoccupation with connectiveness that is, interestingly, recapitulated in the plot of the tale, based as it is on mysterious, or partially known, relationships (Theodore to Jerome, Theodore to Alfonso, the knight of the gigantic sabre to Isabella), and in its imagery, which revolves (as Walpole's distorted epigraph from Homer suggests) around the fragmentation of a body that achieves wholeness at the story's end. Such a concern was also notable in Walpole's epistolary and conversational style. Macaulay noted of Walpole's letters that he 'perpetually startles us by the ease with which he yokes together ideas between which there would seem, at first sight, to be no connexion'.[63] Pinkerton, too, praised Walpole for his 'brilliant fancy, and rapid association of ideas'.[64] This same exuberance is seen in *The Castle of Otranto*, in which, curiously, no scene ever realizes full closure until the end. The story's parts, rather, are linked by prepositions and clauses that stress a hectic simultaneity of movement: 'meanwhile', 'in the meantime', 'while', 'during', 'no sooner', 'that instant'. Chapter divisions seem fortuitous; Walpole's favorite unit of composition is smaller: it is the open-ended incident of the pursuit, the escape, or the supernatural visitation that raises (but does not yet answer) questions that Walpole seems most inclined towards in *The Castle of Otranto*.

Related to this interest in rapid narrative movement and the fragmented (or incomplete) story unit is Walpole's interest in interruption as a device to generate suspense and to heighten

[62] See R. Kiely, *The Romantic Novel in England* (Cambridge, Mass., 1972), p. 41.

[63] Macaulay, Review of *Letters of Horace Walpole,* 239.

[64] Pinkerton, *Walpoliana,* i. xlviii.

the reader's sense of frenetic activity. When conversations are broken at crucial moments (such as at the death of the hermit, or during Jerome's explanation to Theodore of his lineage), the reader is hurried from one incident to the next with irresistible force, his attention engaged by suspended fragments of narration which, in accordance with Walpole's epigraph to the second edition, will, he hopes, eventually be 'assigned to a single shape'.[65] Another, more significant consequence of the speed and fragmentation of narration in Walpole's novel is a serious reduction of emphasis on the internal lives of his characters. Detailed exploration of a character's mind would tend to slow Walpole's narrative and interrupt the momentum of his plot; only by acting in expected, or formulaic, ways can Walpole's characters keep pace with the story he wants to tell. The figures the reader learns most about, Jerome and Hippolita, have a habit of prolonging conversations and arresting movement, a narrative state Walpole is working actively against in *The Castle of Otranto*. Consequently, we are deflected repeatedly from looking into characters in any detail. Two techniques are used to forestall such investigations: Walpole tends to take short cuts in developing a character's personality, and he consistently substitutes exaggeration for depth.

CHARACTER

In his treatment of Theodore, a virtuous character, Walpole composes a number of speeches that show the youth's upright, honest nature. He answers Manfred's questions scrupulously and fairly and submits to his expected punishment with dignity. What certifies Theodore's virtue, however, repeatedly, is his resemblance to Alfonso in the portrait. His person is 'noble, handsome and commanding', the exact resemblance of Alfonso's in the picture gallery; '. . . with the helmet on,' Matilda tells Isabella, 'he is the very image of that picture'.[66] Manfred, too, is 'troubled with the resemblance of Theodore to Alfonso's portrait' and is struck with astonishment and terror when he sees Theodore in armour: 'What, is not that Alfonso? . . . dost thou not see him?' he cries to Hippolita.[67] In reiterating the

[65] *The Castle of Otranto*, p. xiii. [66] Ibid., 52; 85. [67] Ibid., 95; 80.

mysterious connection between Theodore and 'Alfonso the Good', the murdered prince of Otranto, Walpole's need to explore the details of his hero's character is neatly curtailed: his resemblance to the portrait, in a pattern that Sedgwick finds characteristic of Gothic fiction,[68] says everything important that need be known about Theodore.

The less we know about a character—or the more quickly we can know it—the more rapidly the plot can move ahead, so not only short cuts but standardized formulas of response are attached to certain characters from the very beginning of the novel. Such a technique also short-circuits character development, for once the reader understands that Hippolita's reaction to stress is unvarying, he tacitly relieves the author of the responsibility of delineating it in any detail—simple repetition of the basic pattern suffices to signal her state of mind. This tendency to standardize or exaggerate becomes, in effect, Walpole's substitute for examining his characters and is perhaps what Walpole means in his first preface by the word 'maintain': 'The characters', he notes, 'are well drawn, and still better maintained.'[69] All the characters in *The Castle of Otranto*—but especially Manfred—are highly exaggerated. Manfred reacts in the same imperious, startled way to every event, utters wrathful imprecations to his servants, wife, and daughter, and defies all powers in their human and superhuman forms. Our sense of Walpole's characters' exaggerated responses derives in part from the emphasis in the novel on the physical and the dramatic, which leads the characters to act out their internal emotions in highly theatrical ways. Frederic's feelings of guilt over his continued pursuit of Matilda are rendered in this fashion: 'Frederic's blood froze in his veins. For some minutes he remained motionless. Then falling prostrate on his face before the altar, he besought the intercession of every saint for pardon. A flood of tears succeeded to this transport; and the image of the beauteous Matilda rushing in spite of him on his thoughts, he lay on the ground in a conflict of penitence and passion.'[70] Manfred, when angered, tends to display his rage in a similarly overt manner, by slamming

[68] E. K. Sedgwick, 'The Character in the Veil: Imagery of the Surface in the Gothic Novel', *PMLA* xcvi (1981), 255–70.

[69] *The Castle of Otranto*, p. 4.

[70] Ibid., 103.

doors, leaving his companions abruptly, or hastening to other parts of the castle. When he discovers it is Matilda he has stabbed, his reaction is dramatically physical: he 'beat[s] his breast, twist[s] his hands in his locks, and endeavour[s] to recover his dagger from Theodore to dispatch himself'.[71]

Walpole's functional attitude towards his characters (his tendency to value plot and remarkable event over character development) is seen most strikingly in his willingness to violate character to move the storyline ahead. Thus, Manfred, introduced as a defiant, heartless tyrant—capable of gazing down on his mangled son without pity, of defaming the gentle Hippolita, and of propositioning his son's intended bride, who utters announcements like 'Heaven nor hell shall impede my designs', and who defies a sacred prophecy in his attempt to secure the princedom of Otranto for his heirs—is described in the first incident with Theodore as 'naturally humane'.[72] He is, in fact, at first inclined to pardon Theodore—who has just helped Isabella to escape by holding the trap door for her. 'Manfred', the narrator explains, 'was not one of those savage tyrants who wanton in cruelty unprovoked. The circumstances of his fortune had given an asperity to his temper, which was naturally humane; and his virtues were always ready to operate, when his passion did not obscure his reason.'[73] Later, in the same scene, Manfred views Theodore 'with surprise and admiration'.[74] As in all of the incidents in which the narrator insists on Manfred's innate gentleness, this description fails to convince, in part because Walpole, fascinated by excess, is only interested in having Manfred act out his passionate side. Walpole errs in thinking that narrative description can overpower dramatic action here; indeed, this shift of Manfred's character is designed precisely to facilitate a new action: it allows the hero Theodore longer time in the castle so that he can be seen by Matilda and eventually claim the principality of Otranto. In an even odder passage, Walpole delineates another change in Manfred's personality. Pushing Hippolita (who has not seen him since the death of their son) rudely from him, 'the cruel prince' flings away in search of Isabella while Hippolita gamely goes off to verify the servants' story of the foot and leg in the great chamber:

[71] Ibid., 104. [72] Ibid., 23; 30. [73] Ibid., 30. [74] Ibid., 33.

> Manfred [the narrator explains], though persuaded, like his wife, that the vision had been no work of fancy, recovered a little from the tempest of mind into which so many strange events had thrown him. Ashamed too of his inhuman treatment of a princess, who returned every injury with new marks of tenderness and duty, he felt returning love forcing itself into his eyes—but not less ashamed of feeling remorse towards one, against whom he was inwardly meditating a yet more bitter outrage, he curbed the yearnings of his heart, and did not dare to lean even towards pity. The next transition of his soul was to exquisite villainy.[75]

The stiffness of Manfred's emotions in this scene and his metamorphosis from a man of gentleness to a remorseless villain are almost comically wooden and abrupt. Walpole here is engaging in a kind of shorthand of character development, apparently in an effort to deepen Manfred's character, but his unwillingness to spend any time investigating (rather than simply stating) the softer sides of his villain's personality leaves his portrait unbelievable. Similar half-hearted attempts to convince us of Manfred's good side occur sporadically before the story's close: Manfred is said at one point to '[revere] the saint-like virtues of Jerome', but a few pages later we see him ordering Jerome around with his usual abruptness: 'Retire, father; this is no business for monks'.[76] Manfred's heart, we are told in the same section of the novel, is 'capable of being touched'; he watches the reunion of Theodore and Jerome with suppressed marks of astonishment.[77] Yet nowhere do we find Manfred enacting this facet of his character in any concrete way. Frederic, similarly, introduced in the story as a man of courage, valour, and dignity, wavers at key points of the narrative to maintain our sense of Isabella's vulnerability. At one point the narrator tells us that the 'weak prince . . . forgot his enmity to Manfred' in the interest of wedding Matilda, a lapse of memory (and priorities) that is astonishing in view of the formal manner in which he has delivered his challenge and the supernatural quality of his mission.[78] Walpole, in effect, needs to have made his characters far more complex than he has done to convince his readers of such emotional instability. Just as abruptly, Frederic changes his tune again after the

[75] Ibid., 35. [76] Ibid., 45; 58. [77] Ibid., 55. [78] Ibid., 92.

appearance of the armoured hand: '. . . keep your daughter,' he commands the surprised Manfred, 'and think no more of Isabella: the judgments already fallen on your house forbid me matching into it.'[79] The cat fight between Matilda and Isabella over Theodore is another uncharacteristic episode. Walpole, clearly interested in introducing another mood into his story, does so at the expense of his characters' integrities, as Matilda and Isabella, warmed by mutual jealousy, charge each other with questions and deliver half-answers that are directly at odds with 'the natural sincerity and candour of their souls'.[80] Even Theodore delivers an impatient and unhabitual rebuke to Frederic, interrupting his solemn recitation of the prophetic verses engraved on the sabre in the wood near Joppa. 'What is there in these lines', he suddenly asks, 'that affects these princesses? Why were they to be shocked by a mysterious delicacy, that has so little foundation?'[81] In each of these cases, the demands of plot or incident (here, the idea is to forestall an explanation of the mysterious warning) take precedence over conservation of character in a manner that later becomes typical of Gothic romance.

EXAGGERATION AND EXCESS

Closely linked with Walpole's inclination to deny his characters depth is his preoccupation with the superficial for special effects. Repeatedly in *The Castle of Otranto*, in a movement that shifts attention from subtle inward investigations of personality to outward manifestations of display, Walpole produces his strongest effects by dilation and exaggeration—by the introduction of huge or shocking objects that often result in the collapse, silencing, or transfixing of a principal character. The pattern repeats itself from the first supernatural event of the narrative, when Conrad is found crushed beneath the giant helmet in the courtyard—a servant appears, speechless and foaming at the mouth; Manfred, viewing the mangled body of his son, is shocked into silence (though of a different kind). Frederic, confronted with the ghostly hermit of the wood of Joppa, goes through the requisite motions of recoil, trembling,

[79] Ibid., 100. [80] Ibid., 85. [81] Ibid., 79.

and collapse. This procedure of astonishing by shock and its accompanying arrest of movement is the only way of gaining the reader's attention in a narrative whose tempo is already so exaggeratedly hectic, and one often sees Walpole escalating the pace with simple verbal dilations that proceed in a fashion that suggests that emotion (and effect) can be quantified through simple reference to the physical. Manfred, contemplating his son beneath the helmet, fixes his eyes on a 'child dashed to pieces', which becomes 'the bleeding mangled remains of the young prince' and then 'the disfigured corpse'.[82] The increasingly horrifying remains of the unfortunate Conrad are meant, one supposes, to provide a more easily accessible analogue (or short cut) to Manfred's increasing hardness of heart. Manfred's confrontation with the youthful Theodore follows a similarly simple pattern of escalation:

> While the ladies were conveying the wretched mother to her bed, Manfred remained in the court, gazing on the ominous casque, and regardless of the crowd which the strangeness of the event had now assembled round him. The few words he articulated tended solely to enquiries, whether any man knew from whence it could have come? Nobody could give him the least information. However, as it seemed to be the sole object of his curiosity, it soon became so to the rest of the spectators, whose conjectures were as absurd and improbable as the catastrophe itself was unprecedented. In the midst of their senseless guesses a young peasant, whom rumour had drawn thither from a neighbouring village, observed that the miraculous helmet was exactly like that on the figure in black marble of Alfonso the Good, one of their former princes, in the church of St. Nicholas. Villain! What sayest thou? cried Manfred, starting from his trance in a tempest of rage, and seizing the young man by the collar: How darest thou utter such treason? Thy life shall pay for it. The spectators, who as little comprehended the cause of the prince's fury as all the rest they had seen, were at a loss to unravel this new circumstance. The young peasant himself was still more astonished, not conceiving how he had offended the prince: yet recollecting himself, with a mixture of grace and humility, he disengaged himself from Manfred's gripe, and then, with an obeisance which discovered more jealousy of innocence, than dismay, he asked with respect, of what he was guilty! Manfred, more enraged at the vigour, however decently exerted, with which the young man had shaken off his hold, than

[82] Ibid., 17.

appeased by his submission, ordered his attendants to seize him, and, if he had not been withheld by his friends whom he had invited to the nuptials, would have poignarded the peasant in their arms.[83]

Walpole's enjoyment of such scenes is clear. As in *Hieroglyphic Tales,* he connects extravagance to imaginative freedom and to the boundary line, which he loves to straddle, between the comic and the tragic. His interest in such excesses may have had some bearing on his decision to dedicate *The Castle of Otranto* to Lady Mary Coke, whom he once described as 'affect-[ing] to give an air of importance to everything she said. She was sententious about a christening, talked with raptures of a pedigree, and shed tears if a Duchess's perroquet was moulting.'[84]

Walpole's fondness for excessive display puts his readers in an unusual position. Though the effect of *The Castle of Otranto* is ultimately comic (reading the work is exhausting *and* fun), Walpole's attitude towards his audience is not entirely conciliating or sympathetic. He is reluctant to clarify the tone of his novel and delights in leading his readers through a story so frenetic that they lack the time (and peace) to examine his motives. Walpole, in essence, creates an aesthetic atmosphere that empowers him, as its designer, to cast ridicule on an audience that does not possess the discrimination (or cynicism) to look askance at the work. Like the hordes who came to his house to view its curiosities, the readers of *The Castle of Otranto*, their minds made necessarily vacant by Walpole's lack of emphasis on subtle discriminations or delineations of character, 'gape and gobble, and gape again', and Walpole encourages that response to his work in very systematic ways. It is, in effect, the only approach to his work that Walpole makes possible, aside from the intimate responses that took his character into consideration, which he sought from his friends. 'It is not everybody', he remarked significantly to Mason in a letter of 17 April 1765, 'that may in this country play the fool with impunity.'[85] *The Castle of Otranto* is, in its exaggerated, frenzied atmosphere of medievalism, romance, and the supernatural,

[83] Ibid., 18–19.

[84] Horace Walpole, *Memoranda Walpoliana* (1761–1799), ed. and with an introd. by W. S. Lewis, Miscellaneous Antiquities, xiii (Farmington, Conn., 1937), p. 10.

[85] Walpole to William Mason, *Correspondence,* xxviii, 6.

Walpole's triumphant assertion of his own privileged immunity from censure, evidence of the tenuous connectedness he had with the 'real' world that was a source in life of his despair, his cynicism, and his solace.

4 Attractive Persecution: *The Mysteries of Udolpho*

Though Walpole's *The Castle of Otranto* and Ann Radcliffe's *The Mysteries of Udolpho* are linked in superficial ways—both novels are set in a 'Gothic' past; both contain scenes of female persecution and pursuit; and both centre obsessively around a castle—such shared properties and themes obscure a deep-seated difference in the two novelists' employment and understanding of the Gothic. Walpole, interested in the Gothic primarily as a vehicle for effects and a way of licensing extravagance and discord of all kinds, sensed, complexly, the refuge that a reliance on excessive display could provide; Radcliffe, whose sensibility made her averse to such external and excessive displays and unwilling to resolve, or exhibit, private difficulties in the public contexts of writing or socializing, uses the Gothic as a means of exploring qualities of feeling that Walpole refused to tap, and of posing, in particular, the question of the relationship of female feelings to female action. Her failure to understand this relationship—which connects her to Walpole and which the paradox of the Gothic perfectly reflects—is exhibited in the conceptual contradictions of her work, which overtly discourages excessive sensibility in favour of fortitude and endurance. Such a formula is explicitly and repeatedly voiced by the novel's moral spokesman, St Aubert, and by the novelist herself. Radcliffe's inability fully to accept this scheme gives rise, as Wylie Sypher's excellent analysis of *The Mysteries of Udolpho* has shown,[1] to tensions in the novel that lend it its distinctive attenuated tone. Whereas Walpole in *The Castle of Otranto* enjoys (and gains immunity from) the exhibition of conceptual discordances, Radcliffe, in *The Mysteries of Udolpho*, seems less pleased (and considerably more confused) by the incompatibility of the values to which she is attracted. She is unable, in short, to reconcile her moral conviction about the rectitude of endurance and her aesthetic

[1] W. Sypher, 'Social Ambiguity in a Gothic Novel', *Partisan Review*, xii (1945), 50–60.

attraction to situations that break down such qualities—a schism that, as theoreticians of the picturesque like Gilpin and Ruskin repeatedly remarked, is endemic to a visual aesthetic that relies primarily upon affective (rather than moral) criteria.

The Gothic, because it extends rather than resolves the tensions between reason and imagination, and fortitude and sensibility, not only fails to settle the central questions of *The Mysteries of Udolpho*; it contributes directly to the production of an aesthetic of loss and deprivation, in which melancholy and suffering become the highest expression of feeling, and in which the abandonment of the self to the weakness of superstition is seen, paradoxically, as a form of emotional heightening and liberation. The attractiveness of loss is suggested in other, more obvious ways in the novel, hinting, troublingly, at a persecutory aesthetic that suggests serious reservations about female action and initiative. Yet rather than use the Gothic to confront such issues, Radcliffe trifles with the reader by encouraging inauthentic responses to inauthentic situations in her distinctive contribution to Gothic fiction: the supernatural *expliqué*. As Kant noted about fear, such manœuvres help to engender a self-conscious response to sensibility that concerns itself with affectivity to a luxurious degree, one that evades the important questions of action by replacing them with an aesthetic code that (like Walpole's) is self-reflective and self-fulfilling. Such an attitude recoils upon the reader in a way that resembles the reaction of Kant's observer of sublime landscape:

> The *astonishment* amounting almost to terror, the awe and thrill of devout feeling, that takes hold of one when gazing upon the prospect of mountains ascending to heaven, deep ravines and torrents raging there, deep-shadowed solitudes that invite to brooding melancholy, and the like—all this, when we are assured of our own safety, is not actual fear. Rather is it an attempt to gain access to it through imagination, for the purpose of feeling the might of this faculty in combining the movement of the mind thereby aroused with its serenity, and of thus being superior to internal and, therefore, to external, nature, so far as the latter can have any bearing upon our feeling of well-being.[2]

[2] Immanuel Kant, *The Critique of Judgement*, trans. J. C. Meredith (Oxford, 1952), pp. 120–1.

MELANCHOLY

It is, perhaps, no surprise that *The Mysteries of Udolpho* should gather its peculiar energy from moments of deprivation, for the novel celebrates and systematically encourages feelings of melancholy, awe, and fear at the expense of happier ones, and the possession of such feelings is a mark of all the worthy characters in Radcliffe's book. St Aubert, though the strongest and most explicit spokesman in the novel for the values of fortitude and control, is marked by a 'pensive melancholy',[3] which he does not hesitate to indulge. Tears—'[the] language of the heart'—are his way of showing pleasure,[4] and he and his wife and daughter communicate by them. Through St Aubert, Radcliffe enunciates her conviction that gentle melancholy is the emotion most akin to refined perceptions, poetic inspiration, and religious awe: St Aubert, Radcliffe notes early in the novel,

> loved the soothing hour, when the last tints of light die away; when the stars, one by one, tremble through æther, and are reflected on the dark mirror of the waters; that hour, which, of all others, inspires the mind with pensive tenderness, and often elevates it to sublime contemplation. When the moon shed her soft rays among the foliage, he still lingered, and his pastoral supper of cream and fruits was often spread beneath it. Then, on the stillness of night, came the song of the nightingale, breathing sweetness, and awakening melancholy.[5]

Radcliffe seems concerned from the earliest chapters of the novel to establish the connection between melancholy feeling, tears, and God: '[P]ensive melancholy', she remarks, '. . . gives to every object a mellower tint, and breathes a sacred charm over all around'.[6] When St Aubert's heart is full, 'he [weeps], and his thoughts [ascend] to the Great Creator',[7] and when Emily thinks of God, 'her eyes [are] filled with tears of awful love and admiration'.[8] Melancholy, as Valancourt exclaims on their journey through France, is a 'delicious' emotion, 'which no person, who had felt it once, would resign for the gayest

[3] Ann Radcliffe, *The Mysteries of Udolpho*, ed. B. Dobrée (London, 1970), p. 2.
[4] Ibid., 60; 4. [5] Ibid., 4–5. [6] Ibid., 28. [7] Ibid., 36.
[8] Ibid., 48.

pleasures. [Scenes inspiring melancholy] waken our best and purest feelings'.[9] The melancholy of the family of St Aubert is given additional attraction in its contrast to the coarseness and frivolity of the Quesnels.[10]

Pensive melancholy is Emily's inheritance from St Aubert: she too loves to wander through the scenes of nature, 'wrapt in a melancholy charm',[11] and her actions and feelings partake of the same gentleness and sensitivity as her father's. St Aubert's only concern is that the 'degree of susceptibility' in her spirits is 'too exquisite to admit of lasting peace',[12] and, indeed, her grief at the death of her father is indulged to the degree that she finally collapses.[13] Yet, as with St Aubert, tears appear to mark every species of fine feeling: Emily weeps when she admits her esteem for Valancourt,[14] again when they separate, and finally when they reunite at the end of the novel. Weeping, indeed, as Radcliffe intimates in a scene in Venice, is the outward confirmation of Emily's purity and of her beauty: 'Hers was the *contour* of a Madona, with the sensibility of a Magdalen; and the pensive uplifted eye, with the tear that glittered on her cheek, confirmed the expression of the character.'[15]

FORTITUDE, RESTRAINT, AND SUFFERING

This connection of extreme sensibility to melancholy, which marks *The Mysteries of Udolpho* with an emotional complexity that is absent in Walpole's *Castle of Otranto*, clearly troubled Radcliffe. Sensing, perhaps, both the masochistic tendency of a system that equated melancholy with the highest kind of feeling and the solipsistic and seductive nature of the emotion, she juxtaposes to this system of aesthetic values (as Sypher has noted) a moral system that devalues sensibility in favour of self-control and fortitude. St Aubert, paradoxically, is the character who most clearly voices his fears about the dangerous qualities of sensitiveness. He notes that Emily's early evidence of sensibility makes her 'interesting', but he instructs her 'to strengthen her mind; to enure her to habits of self-command; to teach her to reject the first impulse of her feelings . . .'[16] On

[9] Ibid., 46. [10] Ibid., 10–11. [11] Ibid., 6. [12] Ibid., 5.
[13] Ibid., 87. [14] Ibid., 108. [15] Ibid., 184. [16] Ibid., 5.

two separate and important occasions—on the death of his wife and on his own deathbed—he instructs Emily on 'the duty of self-command' and warns her about the enervation of mind that is the result of an improper indulgence of sorrow.[17] Such speeches, with their careful rhetorical balance and their gravity of tone, stand at the moral centre of the novel, and they are balanced at the story's end by Signora Laurentini's impassioned warnings about governing the emotions. 'Above all, my dear Emily,' St Aubert cautions his child,

> 'do not indulge in the pride of fine feeling, the romantic error of amiable minds. Those, who really possess sensibility, ought early to be taught, that it is a dangerous quality, which is continually extracting the excess of misery, or delight, from every surrounding circumstance. And, since, in our passage through this world, painful circumstances occur more frequently than pleasing ones, and since our sense of evil is, I fear, more acute than our sense of good, we become the victims of our feelings, unless we can in some degree command them.'[18]

St Aubert, importantly, advocates not an annihilation of feelings (for 'nothing can be hoped from an insensible [heart]'),[19] but their control, an admonition uttered more violently by the dying Signora Laurentini at the novel's close. 'Remember, sister,' she warns Emily, 'that the passions are the seeds of vices as well as of virtues, from which either may spring, accordingly as they are nurtured. Unhappy they who have never been taught the art to govern them!'[20] Signora Laurentini, tortured by remorse and driven mad by her crimes, presents here a negative version of St Aubert's early speech, and proves the rectitude of his code: she dies at the end, 'a dreadful victim to unresisted passion'.[21]

Such cautions about self-command and restraint are pertinent, for Emily's ordeal at Udolpho tests these qualities to the fullest. Emily's trial, indeed, is one of endurance. 'I can endure with fortitude,' she says to Montoni in a rare moment of confrontation, 'when it is in resistance of oppression'.[22] 'You speak like a heroine', Montoni replies; 'we shall see whether you can

[17] Ibid., 20–1. [18] Ibid., 79–80. [19] Ibid., 20. [20] Ibid., 647.

[21] Ibid., 659. For a detailed discussion of Radcliffe's reservations about sensibility, see N. C. Smith, 'Sense, Sensibility and Ann Radcliffe', *Studies in English Literature*, xiii (1973), 577–90.

[22] *The Mysteries of Udolpho*, p. 381.

suffer like one.'[23] One of the deepest problems with fortitude is that it may become a doctrine advocating a dangerous kind of passivity, a system of defence that discourages action of any kind. Emily, pursued by Count Morano, locked in a turret, defrauded of her estates, awaits 'the events of futurity' with 'meek patience'.[24] Emily's passivity is, obviously, necessary for the story to move ahead, but there are signs that Radcliffe approves of this puzzling inaction on other grounds. Madame Montoni, for example, though Emily counsels her to relinquish her settlement and give up her ideas of escape,[25] struggles actively and ineffectually against the persecutions of Montoni and her active side seems linked directly with her demise: her resistance leads eventually to her imprisonment and death.

The impropriety of acting in *The Mysteries of Udolpho*—in a world that, as St Aubert admits early in the novel, is more painful than pleasing[26]—guarantees that heroism (in Montoni's sarcastic formulation) will depend on suffering. And if painful events do not impinge on the heroine from the outside (embodied, for example, in a Montoni or a Morano) they can, complexly, be generated from within, not only by a melancholic dwelling on the past but by an attitude of passivity dictated by an adherence to the doctrine of fortitude. When Emily selflessly refuses to marry Valancourt out of fear of involving him in lasting distresses (and out of trepidation about the indecorousness of an elopement), she commits a double error: devaluing her unprotected state and ignoring her own ominous intuitions about Montoni (intuitions that Valancourt's report corroborates), she concludes sophistically that there is not enough proof of her guardian's evil nature and, '[distrusting] the fallacies of passion',[27] dismisses the rumour of Montoni's villainy as unfounded.[28] Later, Valancourt calls this action by its right name: it is 'an absurd and criminal delicacy'[29] that Emily allowed herself to be taken to Italy instead of marrying him. Yet, repeatedly, Emily (with Ann Radcliffe's approval)

[23] Ibid., 381. [24] Ibid., 418. [25] Ibid., 310–11. [26] Ibid., 80.

[27] Ibid., 158.

[28] She repeats this error with the treacherous porter Barnardine. The man's 'unpleasant air and countenance' and his suspicious actions suggest that he designs to draw her into danger, 'but a little reflection shewed her the improbability of this' (ibid., 333). A few pages later, he lures her with the promise of seeing Madame Montoni into the turret and locks her in.

[29] Ibid., 292.

retreats in this way into social decorums as a way of relieving herself from acting. Out of 'delicacy' she does not question La Voisin about the Marquis de Villeroi though she has reason to believe that her father has a mysterious connection to the family.[30] 'Duty' causes her to consign St Aubert's papers to the flames, an act that destroys forever (it appears) the possibility of uncovering the truth about her father's involvement with a dreadful deed—and Ann Radcliffe's endorsement of this decision is clear; she calls the alternative a 'delusion'.[31] Her hesitation to question servants about Udolpho, Montoni, or Morano stems from 'an unwillingness to ask unnecessary questions, and to mention family concerns to a servant'[32]—an unwillingness that seems unbelievable in view of her involvement with Montoni. Indeed, Emily's actions appear, perplexingly, to extend her punishment—aware of the impropriety of listening at the door of her aunt's room, she leaves without hearing anything about her situation at the castle. In the extraordinary scene in which Morano visits her room at night, she pointedly fails to question him about Montoni, though he gives ample evidence that he knows his character and is privy to his plans for Emily. When Emily is taken to Tuscany and is befriended by the daughter of Montoni's agents, who receive her in their cottage, she refuses to ask the girl about Montoni's designs: she 'disdained', Radcliffe writes, 'to tempt the innocent girl to a conduct so mean, as that of betraying the private conversation of her parents'.[33] Most complexly, perhaps, she fails to enquire in any depth into the conduct of Valancourt when he returns to her, his character maligned by rumours of dissipation and infidelity, rumours that her heart explicitly rejects. Radcliffe in such cases sacrifices her heroine's comfort to the demands of plot or minor morals—prohibiting her to arrest the progress of events by acting, she elevates passivity into an ethical system and drives the burden of suffering back onto her characters: '. . . for whatever I may be reserved,' as Emily reminds herself in the middle of the novel, 'let me, at least, avoid self-reproach'.[34]

[30] Ibid., 87. [31] Ibid., 103. [32] Ibid., 235. [33] Ibid., 418.

[34] Ibid., 251. Such a conflict is exacerbated (as in many Gothic novels) by Radcliffe's insistence on making points about social behaviour in situations that demand a broader ethical view.

Emily's tendency to cling to social and moral values in distinctly non-social and non-moral contexts (as at Udolpho, where prostitutes are entertained, accusations of murder are given, and wine-glasses shatter from poisoned drink) gives rise to a kind of extreme moral isolation that itself can be enervating and destructive. Because she decorously (and selflessly) avoids implicating others (Madame Montoni's servant Annette, Madame Montoni, and Maddelina, the daughter of Montoni's Tuscan agents) in her own distresses, she has no one with whom to share the weight of her sufferings (and her knowledge). She alone must keep the secret of the veiled picture and of the corpse in the turret (is it the body of Madame Montoni?) and her reason, not unexpectedly, 'seemed to totter under the intolerable weight'.[35] The garrulous Annette, who cannot keep any secret, is a striking contrast to Emily, who keeps secrets even from herself. Indeed, Emily, guided by St Aubert's dictates of fortitude and self-command, has a tendency to suppress knowledge, a procedure that Radcliffe imitates in conscious and unconscious ways in the novel. She, too, vexingly, keeps the secret of what is behind the black veil: the mystery is not revealed until the story's end. More complexly, she fails to deal in any systematic way with Emily's unconscious fascination with Montoni. Towards the middle of her imprisonment, and grouped densely within two chapters, there are hints of Emily's attraction to the striking Montoni. Gazing out the window of the castle, she observes a party of horsemen dressed in uniform and bearing daggers, and hopes, 'she scarcely knew why, that Montoni would accompany the party'.[36] At dinner the following day, she analyses his countenance with veiled admiration, and after the fracas following his attempted poisoning, the belief of Montoni's death gives Emily's spirits 'a sudden shock, and she grew faint as she saw him in imagination, expiring at her feet'.[37] Emily's possible attraction to Montoni extends (and deepens) the occasional parallels between her situation and that of Richardson's Clarissa, whom she in some respects resembles and whose story her abduction to Udolpho some-

[35] Ibid., 350. In such instances, as Daniel Cottom has noted, decorum and hysteria become, 'in effect, identical' (*The Civilized Imagination: A Study of Ann Radcliffe, Jane Austen, and Sir Walter Scott* (Cambridge, 1985), p. 59).

[36] Ibid., 302

[37] Ibid., 316.

times recalls. But such moral and amorous complexities are not purposeful in *The Mysteries of Udolpho*: indeed, Radcliffe (following the lead of her heroine) quickly stifles such insights, causing Emily some chapters later to fall into a decline approaching a kind of temporary madness provoked by her distresses and her isolation. Emily's deepest fears are not, interestingly, allowed an explicit outlet in *The Mysteries of Udolpho*—rather, they take a poetic turn, being released in sonnets about violent death and bloody deeds.[38] Emily's fainting throughout *The Mysteries of Udolpho* evidences the extraordinary burden of the secret knowledge she bears and the extent to which she must internalize her fears. Fortitude here takes on the qualities of masochism: unable to erase her ability to feel, Emily must experience acutely all the pain of deprivation; unable to act, she must suffer or suppress her knowledge of impending suffering. Jane Austen's solution to such problems of hysterical internalization in *Northanger Abbey* (her corrective to *Udolpho*) was talk—the rational sharing of information in a social context[39]—a solution denied Emily because of her solitude.

DEBILITY AND LOSS

The complexity of the Gothic in *The Mysteries of Udolpho* is that it exalts this suffering aesthetically, and provides its heroine with an ability to escape (temporarily) the constrictions of her situation. Emily's 'Gothic' responses are reactive, not active—not one of the supernatural events in *The Mysteries of Udolpho* is, finally, real—and Radcliffe, by using the Gothic, thus skirts the problem of action by concentrating interest on the approach to the terrifying moment and on the heroine's apprehension of it. Conveniently, it functions in contexts of loss and deprivation; in her happier days, Emily, Radcliffe says explicitly, would not have been alarmed by the fancies of superstition[40] and, indeed, the reader hardly anticipates the return of ghosts and spirits after the marriage of Emily and Valancourt. This is a problem of some magnitude: the Gothic,

[38] See, for example, 'The Pilgrim', ibid., 415.

[39] See R. Kiely, *The Romantic Novel in England* (Cambridge, Mass., 1972), pp. 118–35.

[40] *The Mysteries of Udolpho*, p. 102.

explicitly, involves feelings that are related to melancholy (which Ann Radcliffe connects to the religious, the poetic, and the sublime) but it is as explicitly a response to persecution and unhappiness. Such a link between persecution and fine feeling generates an aesthetic of loss or of suffering that has interesting ramifications for Ann Radcliffe's peculiar style of Gothic and for the reader (and enjoyer) of such fiction.

Radcliffe is insistent throughout *The Mysteries of Udolpho* that the experience of the Gothic is connected with debility, infirmity, and the loss of reason. Emily, hearing about the music near the Convent of St Clair, 'though she smiled at the mention of this ridiculous superstition, could not, in the present tone of her spirits, wholly resist its contagion'.[41] When she experiences terror in the library at La Vallée, her reason is 'dissipated',[42] and on her fears in her father's bedchamber, Radcliffe explains,

> The solitary life, which Emily had led of late, and the melancholy subjects, on which she had suffered her thoughts to dwell, had rendered her at times sensible to the 'thick-coming fancies' of a mind greatly enervated. It was lamentable, that her excellent understanding should have yielded, even for a moment, to the reveries of superstition, or rather to those starts of imagination, which deceive the senses into what can be called nothing less than momentary madness. Instances of this temporary failure of mind had more than once occurred since her return home; particularly when, wandering through this lonely mansion in the evening twilight, she had been alarmed by appearances, which would have been unseen in her more cheerful days.[43]

Her superstitious fancies are a 'weakness'[44] for which she scolds Annette.

Radcliffe's insistent connection of imaginary superstitions with weakness (or even madness), and her provoking tendency to warn her readers against them even as she excites their imagination with her powerful descriptions of Emily's reactions, point to a central paradox of the Gothic mode. Though superstitious terror is 'dreadful' and 'pitiable',[45] it is also, importantly, aesthetically provocative and valuable. About the veiled picture, Radcliffe writes, 'a terror of this nature, as

[41] Ibid., 68. [42] Ibid., 95. [43] Ibid., 102.
[44] Ibid., 103; 232; 355; 392; 530; 635. [45] Ibid., 103.

it occupies and expands the mind, and elevates it to high expectation, is purely sublime, and leads us, by a kind of fascination, to seek even the object, from which we appear to shrink'.[46] The language of religious emotion ('expand', 'elevate') recurs in later passages in the novel: she speaks of 'that love, so natural to the human mind, of whatever is able to distend its faculties with wonder and astonishment'.[47] Such imagery of expansion, distention, and elevation hints at the release that superstitious terrors can bring to the harassed mind. Imprisoned at Udolpho, Emily gains access to another (supernatural) world through her fears; weakness becomes, paradoxically, a peculiar source of energy, an energy denied her in 'real' life.

Such a loss-related aesthetic is in keeping with the conservative emphasis of the book.[48] La Vallée, itself a landscape of loss, a place where, as Radcliffe notes, Emily 'could weep unobserved, retrace [her parents'] steps, and remember each minute particular of their manners'[49]—becomes a symbol of an unattainable (but none the less fervently desired) past, a locus of loss that is itself forever lost. In situating the truest human values of the novel in the past (as St Aubert does and as Emily does by revering the memory of her parents and of Valancourt), Radcliffe suggests the unsettling possibility that loss is necessary for fine feeling. Like melancholy (which is the expression of loss), loss thus becomes desirable and can be artificially generated (or extended) (which Radcliffe does by establishing a moral code prohibiting female action).[50] The weakness of succumbing to Gothic terrors is punished by humiliation—it is Emily's dog, Manchon, not a ghost, who brushes against Emily in the dark;[51] it is a pirate, not the dead Marchioness de Villeroi, whose face rises above the counterpane at Chateau-le-Blanc.[52] This is the crux of the problem of

[46] Ibid., 248.

[47] Ibid., 549.

[48] See D. Durant, 'Ann Radcliffe and the Conservative Gothic', *Studies in English Literature,* xxii (1982), 519–30.

[49] *The Mysteries of Udolpho,* p. 98.

[50] For an 'active' female like Eaton Stannard Barrett's self-styled heroine of romance, Cherry Wilkinson, the solution is more straightforward: 'since adversity . . . encreases virtue,' she remarks, 'it must be a virtue to seek adversity' (*The Heroine, or Adventures of Cherubina,* 2nd edn. (3 vols., London, 1814), ii. 187).

[51] *The Mysteries of Udolpho,* p. 96.

[52] Ibid., 635.

the Gothic in Ann Radcliffe's work: interested in the affective powers of the supernatural while systematically denying its existence, the reader of her narratives feels confused and cheated.[53] Thrust back upon the luxury of feeling for its own sake, he enacts, for the pleasure of fear, the aesthetic victimization that is his tenuous point of contact with the sensitive Emily St Aubert.

[53] Both Scott and Talfourd commented on this tendency. 'A stealthy step behind the arras', wrote Scott, 'may doubtless, in some situations, and when the nerves are tuned to a certain pitch, have no small influence upon the imagination; but if the conscious listener discovers it to be only the noise made by the cat, the solemnity of the feeling is gone, and the visionary is at once angry with his senses for having been cheated, and with his reason for having acquiesced in the deception' ([Sir Walter Scott], 'Prefatory Memoir to Mrs Ann Radcliffe', in *The Novels of Mrs Ann Radcliffe*, Ballantyne's Novelist's Library, x (London, 1824), xxvi). Talfourd, who accused Radcliffe of 'turning traitor' to her own potent art, made a similar observation: 'Grant only the possibility of [the] truth [of the supernatural] . . . and there is nothing extravagant in the whole machinery, by which it works. But discard it altogether, and introduce, in its stead, a variety of startling phenomena, which are resolved at last into petty deceptions and gross improbabilities, and you at once disappoint the fancy, and shock the understanding of the reader' ([T. N. Talfourd], 'Memoir of the Life and Writings of Mrs Radcliffe', in *Gaston de Blondeville, or The Court of Henry III. Keeping Festival in Ardenne, A Romance.—St. Alban's Abbey, A Metrical Tale; With Some Poetical Pieces. By Anne Radcliffe* (4 vols., London, 1826), i. 115–16). Such objections are a recurring feature of early criticisms of her novels. See also [Samuel Taylor Coleridge], Review of *The Mysteries of Udolpho*, in the *Critical Review*, 2nd ser., xi (1794), 362; repr. in *Coleridge's Miscellaneous Criticism*, ed. T. M. Raysor (Cambridge, Mass., 1936), p. 357.

5 Cross-purposes: *The Monk*

When, in the course of the Procession of St Clare, the Mother St Ursula mounts the dazzling throne of St Clare and reveals the extent of the Prioress's crimes against Agnes, she voices what appears to be one of the main themes of *The Monk*: 'Mine', she says, 'is the task to rend the veil from Hypocrisy, and show misguided Parents to what dangers the Woman is exposed, who falls under the sway of a monastic Tyrant.'[1] Lorenzo, a few pages earlier and using the same language of unmasking and revelation, contemplates the procession with the same urge to expose the hypocrite and enlighten a populace too easily duped by the semblance of virtue:

> Conscious that among those who chaunted the praises of their God so sweetly, there were some who cloaked with devotion the foulest sins, their hymns inspired him with detestation at their Hypocrisy. He had long observed with disapprobation and contempt the superstition, which governed Madrid's Inhabitants. His good sense had pointed out to him the artifices of the Monks, and the gross absurdity of their miracles, wonders, and supposititious reliques. He blushed to see his Countrymen the Dupes of deceptions so ridiculous, and only wished for an opportunity to free them from their monkish fetters. That opportunity, so long desired in vain, was at length presented to him. He resolved not to let it slip, but to set before the People in glaring colours, how enormous were the abuses but too frequently practised in Monasteries, and how unjustly public esteem was bestowed indiscriminately upon all who wore a religious habit. He longed for the moment destined to unmask the Hypocrites, and convince his Country men, that a sanctified exterior does not always hide a virtuous heart.[2]

Lewis's adoption of the language and imagery of masking throughout *The Monk* suggests his association of vice and concealment, his conviction that to the innocent 'Vice is ever most

[1] Matthew Lewis, *The Monk: A Romance*, ed. H. Anderson (London, 1973), p. 350.
[2] Ibid., 345–6.

dangerous when lurking behind the Mask of Virtue'.[3] Ambrosio's crimes (as the title of Lewis's novel suggests) are more heinous because of his public stature, because of his insistence on retaining the outward semblance of goodness despite his inward corruption. As Lewis explains of Ambrosio after his commerce with Matilda,

> . . . what He wanted in purity of heart, He supplied by exterior sanctity. The better to cloak his transgression, He redoubled his pretensions to the semblance of virtue, and never appeared more devoted to Heaven as since He had broken through his engagements. Thus did He unconsciously add Hypocrisy to perjury and incontinence; He had fallen into the latter errors from yielding to seduction almost irresistible; But he was now guilty of a voluntary fault by endeavouring to conceal those, into which Another had betrayed him.[4]

Ambrosio's duplicity, indeed, becomes one of his major offences against heaven: in the scene following the rape of Antonia, where he raves at the extent of his crimes, he proclaims himself 'an Hypocrite', 'a perjured Hypocrite', before he names himself 'an Assassin', a 'Ravisher, a Betrayer, a Monster of cruelty, lust, and ingratitude',[5] and hypocrisy is the first sin with which the devil charges him at the novel's end.[6] Because criminality and concealment are associated in this way, it is not surprising to find that the moral impetus of the novel is that of unmasking, of exposing, and revealing. Elvira's threats to Ambrosio when she discovers him at Antonia's bedside predict the Monk's eventual and proper fate: 'I will unmask you, Villain . . . Your iniquity shall be unveiled to the public eye'.[7] Satan's revelation of Ambrosio's sins—'Hark, Ambrosio, while I unveil your crimes!'[8]—is tendered in the same terms of unmasking.

Associated with this apparent condemnation of disguise is another of the novel's main themes, which projects the plea for openness onto an emotional scale, a theme that was to function prominently in Lewis's later works: that of sympathy or mercy.

[3] Ibid., 84. For more on this emphasis on concealing, see I. Trostaniecki, 'La poétique du caché dans *Le moine* de M. G. Lewis', *Recherches anglaises et américaines*, vi (1973), 43–59.

[4] *The Monk*, p. 226.

[5] Ibid., 385.

[6] Ibid., 440.

[7] Ibid., 301–2.

[8] Ibid., 439.

One of Ambrosio's greatest faults is his severity—at first the manifestation of his need to suppress his own passionate nature, it is later transferred onto others (most notably, Agnes and Antonia) first as a lack of human feeling, an unwillingness to excuse the faults of others,[9] and then as sadism. Ambrosio's outer rigour, as Matilda knows, augments as his inner weakness grows. She warns him that to show compassion towards Agnes, to beg for a mitigation of her sentence, would be to create a suspicion of his own weakness and she thus advises him to 'redouble your outward austerity, and thunder out menaces against the errors of others, the better to conceal your own. . . . She is unworthy to enjoy Love's pleasures, who has not wit enough to conceal them.'[10]

When Ambrosio, detected in Antonia's bedroom, sues for mercy, Elvira refuses to grant it and causes the Monk to commit one of his most unforgivable crimes: that of murder. 'Inhumanity' (one of the words emblazoned on his forehead in Lorenzo's fearful dream and a crime attributed to him by the Fiend at the novel's end)[11] is the dominating passion of all the novel's worst characters and eventually rebounds on the villains' own heads: the cruel Prioress is sacrificed to the fury of the mob, the selfish Donna Rodolpho breaks a blood-vessel in a fit of rage, and Ambrosio suffers eternal damnation. Even Elvira (though marked out early as one of Lewis's most prominent victims) is made to die for her rash withholding of mercy.

Though, at the end, pardon for Ambrosio is still theologically possible (God's mercy, as he knows, is infinite and 'the Penitent shall meet his forgiveness', and the arrival of the guards with his pardon symbolically suggests that this is true),[12] the issue is complicated by the monstrousness of the Friar's crimes and the excess of despair which he indulges in his prison cell. Ambrosio's relinquishment of his hope for mercy is the devil's greatest triumph: from the moment he signs the contract, he is 'the God-abandoned': 'You have given up your claim to mercy,' the devil tells him, 'and nothing can restore to you the rights which you have foolishly resigned.'[13] Ambrosio's failure to recognize the possibility of forgiveness brings his crime against Agnes symbolically back on himself: once having

[9] Ibid., 22. [10] Ibid., 231. [11] Ibid., 18; 440. [12] Ibid., 434.
[13] Ibid., 437; 440.

refused pity to a frail human, he now inadvertently denies it to himself. The address to the 'Haughty Lady', which Lewis added to all editions of *The Monk* after the first, underlines the need for man to exercise both self-reflection and compassion:

> Haughty Lady, why shrank you back when yon poor frail-one drew near? Was the air infected by her errors? Was your purity soiled by her passing breath? Ah! Lady, smooth that insulting brow: stifle the reproach just bursting from your scornful lip: wound not a soul that bleeds already! She has suffered, suffers still. Her air is gay, but her heart is broken; her dress sparkles, but her bosom groans. Lady, to look with mercy on the conduct of others, is a virtue no less than to look with severity on your own.[14]

To approve Agnes's demand for mercy is to accept that man is frail and subject to temptation. Ambrosio's refusal to tender forgiveness is thus also a statement about his pride, about his buried conviction that man is on a level with angels, that human weakness should not only not be pitied but ideally should not exist.

If the moral message of Lewis's book seems bound up with the virtue of compassion and the knowledge of man's frailty—humanistic themes that would figure in Lewis's later tragedies—and the resolution of the narrative seems to depend on a process of revelation and unmasking, such urges are offset by another pattern of images and an aesthetic procedure that carry equal (if more subversive) weight: those of veiling and distancing. Though openness appears to be the moral desideratum of Lewis's book, a fascination with indirection, transference, and distancing marks *The Monk,* and dictates, ultimately, its aesthetic appeal; an interest in psychological and aesthetic deflection replaces the apparent call for openness and the demand for pity is fulfilled by the creation of erotic scenes that encourage a debased form of sympathy: a kind of prurient curiosity that depends upon withdrawal and distance.

VEILS AND VOYEURISM

When Antonia enters the novel in Chapter I, Lewis's emphasis on her half-concealed beauty encourages the reader to view her

[14] Ibid., 453.

(as, uncomfortably, Ambrosio later will) in a slightly salacious light. Though the cavaliers wish fervently to see her face, they are denied that satisfaction:

Her features were hidden by a thick veil; But struggling through the crowd had deranged it sufficiently to discover a neck which for symmetry and beauty might have vied with the Medicean Venus. It was of the most dazzling whiteness, and received additional charms from being shaded by the tresses of her long fair hair, which descended in ringlets to her waist. . . . Her bosom was carefully veiled. Her dress was white . . . and just permitted to peep out from under it a little foot of the most delicate proportions.[15]

Lewis's emphasis on veils in delineating Antonia's character has a number of repercussions: not only does it mark her as a victim, insufficiently protected in a giant crowd (Leonella later commands her to remove her headcovering), but it suggests that the attention that she will (inadvertently) draw upon herself will be specifically sexual in character. More troublingly, as Antonia is indeed the novel's most virtuous and beautiful character, it suggests a standard of beauty (or of aesthetic interest) that is distinctly erotic, based upon imaginative projection and partial concealment. In the scene following Ambrosio's sermon, Lorenzo and Christoval linger in the church to see the faces of the nuns of St Clare, who will unveil when they enter the holy sanctuary:

'Oh! Lorenzo, we shall see such a glorious sight! [exclaims Christoval] . . . the Prioress of St. Clare, the better to escape the gaze of such impure eyes as belong to yourself and your humble Servant, thinks proper to bring her holy flock to confession in the Dusk . . . There is news for you, you Rogue! We shall see some of the prettiest faces in Madrid!'[16]

The sexual connotations of veiling and unveiling reach a height in the figure of Rosario, whose face, at first 'continually muffled up in his Cowl'[17] and whose body, shrouded by his habit, excite the Monk with desire by the partial glimpses they reveal of a female form:

As She uttered these last words, She lifted her arm, and made a motion as if to stab herself. The Friar's eyes followed with dread the

[15] Ibid., 9. [16] Ibid., 30–1. [17] Ibid., 42.

course of the dagger. She had torn open her habit, and her bosom was half exposed. The weapon's point rested upon her left breast: And Oh! that was such a breast! The Moon-beams darting full upon it, enabled the Monk to observe its dazzling whiteness. His eye dwelt with insatiable avidity upon the beauteous Orb. A sensation till then unknown filled his heart with a mixture of anxiety and delight: A raging fire shot through every limb; The blood boiled in his veins, and a thousand wild wishes bewildered his imagination.[18]

When Matilda plays the harp as Ambrosio lies on his sickbed, he notices that her cowl has fallen back:

Two coral lips were visible, ripe, fresh, and melting, and a Chin in whose dimples seemed to lurk a thousand Cupids. Her Habit's long sleeve would have swept along the Chords of the Instrument: To prevent this inconvenience She had drawn it above her elbow, and by this means an arm was discovered formed in the most perfect symmetry, the delicacy of whose skin might have contended with snow in whiteness. Ambrosio dared to look on her but once . . . Every beauty which He had seen, appeared embellished, and those still concealed Fancy represented to him in glowing colours.[19]

The deliberate and repeated sensual orientation of *The Monk* (whether Lewis is describing scenes of sexuality or of punishment), combined with incidents in which physical beauty is associated with a form of excited or confused withdrawal,[20] puts the reader in the novel's most crucial moments in the position of a voyeur, watching curiously (as in the scene in which Lorenzo and Christoval await the nuns) from afar. The episode in which Ambrosio, gazing in the magic mirror, sees Antonia preparing for her bath thus becomes an analogue to the reader's relationship to the novel: his moral sense weakened by the sensual scene before him and guided by Ambrosio's excessive response, he reacts with a strange mixture of prurient curiosity and helpless pity for Antonia. Lewis's willingness repeatedly to expose his heroine in this way adds to the unhealthy atmosphere:

[18] Ibid., 65.

[19] Ibid., 78.

[20] L'Epine's engraving (after Lafitte) of Ambrosio looking uneasily from his bed at Matilda singing beside him (*The Monk: A Romance* (3 vols., Paris, 1807), frontispiece) is in this respect more responsive to Lewis's view of eroticism than the frontispiece to the Paris, 1798 translation that shows Matilda baring her breasts.

The scene was a small closet belonging to her apartment. She was undressing to bathe herself. The long tresses of her hair were already bound up. The amorous Monk had full opportunity to observe the voluptuous contours and admirable symmetry of her person. She threw off her last garment, and advancing to the Bath prepared for her, She put her foot into the water. It struck cold, and She drew it back again. Though unconscious of being observed, an in-bred sense of modesty induced her to veil her charms; and She stood hesitating upon the brink, in the attitude of the Venus de Medicis. At this moment a tame Linnet flew towards her, nestled its head between her breasts, and nibbled them in wanton play. The smiling Antonia strove in vain to shake off the Bird, and at length raised her hands to drive it from its delightful harbour. Ambrosio could bear no more: His desires were worked up to phrenzy.

'I yield!' He cried, dashing the mirror upon the ground: 'Matilda, I follow you! Do with me what you will!'[21]

Matilda's presence in this episode creates a triangulated structure that contributes to the reader's sense of himself as voyeur. Matilda both neutrally facilitates the scene (as purveyor of the magic mirror and thus as an analogue to the author, Lewis) and functions as a kind of moral procuress. She is an individual with whom the reader can have no sympathy, especially given her perverted emotional relationship to Ambrosio in the scene. Ambrosio's heated response to the picture, which explicitly echoes his sexual language to Matilda in earlier moments—'I yield! . . . Matilda, I follow you! Do with me what you will!' (a response that, interestingly, shows Matilda, not Antonia, to be the true temptress)—confuses sexual scene and response to such a degree that the reader is hurried through the episode without, perhaps, the opportunity to formulate a moral judgement—either about Lewis or perhaps about himself for his reaction to the event. Lewis also cunningly infuses Ambrosio's vocabulary into the description of Antonia so the reader is encouraged to share his physiological (non-moral) reaction: her 'contours' are called 'voluptuous' and the linnet's harbour between her breasts adjudged 'delightful'.

[21] *The Monk*, p. 271.

DEFLECTIONS OF SYMPATHY

This unkind toying with his characters is noticeable throughout *The Monk* and is one of the chief barriers to the kind of sympathetic identification of reader and character that Lewis establishes as the prerequisite for mercy. The characters with whom we most readily sympathize, in fact—Antonia and Agnes—undergo punishments so extreme as to excite horror rather than pity, and Antonia from the moment of her appearance in the book is delineated as a victim of such remarkable passivity as to rule out the complex identification that true sympathy requires: brought unwillingly into the crowded church by her insensitive aunt, she immediately expresses a sensation of constriction and fear and a wish to retire: 'By all means, Leonella, let us return home immediately; The heat is excessive, and I am terrified at such a crowd.'[22] As they will with Ambrosio, her fear and her modesty produce an explicitly sexual response: the two cavaliers start from their seats and chivalrously offer them to the ladies. The symbolic unveiling of the unwilling Antonia ('it is not the custom in Murcia', she protests to Leonella) and Leonella's unmeditated exposure of her name and circumstances in a public place serve further to mark her as a victim, a person to whom things are done. Both Lorenzo's dream, in which she is tortured by the caresses of a gigantic monster upon the altar, and the gypsy's song, which singles her out as a victim of destruction, make it difficult to see Antonia as in any way responsible for or effective in determining her fate, and her giddy dismissal of the gipsy's predictions after a few hours makes it clear that Lewis has no intention of delineating a character with subtle or believable emotions.

The reader's relationship to Antonia is also complicated by the fact that Lewis often treats her in comic or sardonic ways at important moments in the narrative. Her violent reaction to Ambrosio's sermon (which can be accounted for by the fact that he is her brother)[23] is rendered in such terms that her response seems to be sexual in nature: 'Antonia, while She gazed upon him eagerly, felt a pleasure fluttering in her bosom

[22] Ibid., 9.

[23] Elvira has a similar heightened reaction to his voice (ibid., 250).

which till then had been unknown to her, and for which She in vain endeavoured to account. She waited with impatience till the Sermon should begin; and when at length the Friar spoke, the sound of his voice seemed to penetrate into her very soul. . . . no other of the Spectators felt such violent sensations as did the young Antonia . . . '[24] Because the consanguinity of Antonia and Ambrosio is a fact initially withheld from the reader and because the Monk has been presented in a markedly sexual way (his eyes are 'fiery and penetrating', his stature 'lofty', and his features 'uncommonly handsome'),[25] and because his entrance has been preceded by a conversation that establishes Antonia's ridiculous *naïveté* about sexual matters (she, like Ambrosio, 'knows not in what consists the difference of Man and Woman'),[26] the reader is forced to attribute Antonia's reactions to amorous interest. A correct response to this purest of characters is thus diverted (or perverted) and Antonia is made to seem attracted (in a pattern of scenes that gains increasing momentum in the novel) to her own eventual rapist and murderer.

In simpler ways, Lewis encourages distance from the very characters for whom he seems to solicit the most sympathy. In the exchange between Lorenzo and Don Christoval that follows the women's departure from the church, Lewis pokes fun at a lover's infatuation and in the process Antonia is made to seem a simpleton:

> 'I should be a Villain [declares Lorenzo], could I think of her on any other terms than marriage; and in truth She seems possessed of every quality requisite to make me happy in a Wife. Young, lovely, gentle, sensible. . . .'
>
> 'Sensible? Why, She said nothing but "Yes," and "No".'
>
> 'She did not say much more, I must confess—But then She always said "Yes," or "No," in the right place.'[27]

Later, Antonia's suppression of her true feelings about Don Christoval's attitude towards her aunt draws a sardonic (and equally misogynistic) comment from Lewis: 'Now Antonia had observed the air, with which Don Christoval had kissed this same hand; But as She drew conclusions from it somewhat different from her Aunt's, She was wise enough to hold her

[24] Ibid., 18. [25] Ibid., 18. [26] Ibid., 17. [27] Ibid., 24–5.

tongue. As this is the only instance known of a Woman's ever having done so, it was judged worthy to be recorded here.'[28] Even more oddly, after the horrific scene of Elvira's death (in which, cruelly, Antonia is made to stumble on her mother's corpse), Lewis cynically remarks, 'Nobody dies of mere grief; Of this Antonia was an instance.'[29] A similar off-hand (and misquoted) comment accompanies Lorenzo's grief at the violent death of Antonia—'Men have died, and worms have eat them; but not for Love!'—a remark particularly unfortunate in light of past scenes of half-corrupted bodies and the coming descriptions of Agnes's decaying baby.[30]

This glib, almost sadistically comic attitude towards his characters is accompanied by a more violently contradictory (and ethically more controversial) tactic. Though *The Monk* appears to be in part about the need for mercy, Lewis as author extends very little mercy to his own characters. Antonia is so obviously and repeatedly the victim—dragged to church, twice nearly ravished by Ambrosio, her mother murdered in her bedroom as she sleeps, and finally violated and then stabbed to death by Ambrosio in the vaults of St Clare—that she seems to invite the same ruthless treatment from her creator as she does from the Monk. Only in the end (when it is too late) does she achieve a certain stature when she represents to Ambrosio the impropriety and danger of being alone with him in the tombs, but even here Lewis represents her as almost ridiculously naïve:

> 'Unhand me, Father!' She cried, her honest indignation tempered by alarm at her unprotected position; 'Why have you brought me to this place? Its appearance freezes me with horror! Convey me from hence, if you have the least sense of pity and humanity! Let me return to the House, which I have quitted I know not how; But stay here one moment longer, I neither will, or ought.'[31]

The Prioress meets a fate at the hands of the populace that, in view of her innocence of Agnes's death and her cries for mercy, must be seen as too severe, yet it follows the same pattern of incredible, almost joyful escalation as does Antonia's end in the vaults. Because Lorenzo, as the ethical representative of

[28] Ibid., 34. [29] Ibid., 308. [30] Ibid., 399; 412–13; 415. [31] Ibid., 382.

restraint in the scene, pities the Domina but cannot control the crowd, Lewis, feigning an inability to combat the mob, wreaks a vengeance upon her that is immensely satisfying while still paying lip service to a system that holds compassion to be the greatest good:

. . . a multitude of voices exclaimed, that the Prioress should be given up to their fury. To this Don Ramirez refused to consent positively. Even Lorenzo bad the People remember, that She had undergone no trial, and advised them to leave her punishment to the Inquisition. All representations were fruitless: The disturbance grew still more violent, and the Populace more exasperated. In vain did Ramirez attempt to convey his Prisoner out of the Throng. Wherever He turned, a band of Rioters barred his passage, and demanded her being delivered over to them more loudly than before. Ramirez ordered his Attendants to cut their way through the multitude: Oppressed by numbers, it was impossible for them to draw their swords. He threatened the Mob with the vengeance of the Inquisition: But in this moment of popular phrenzy even this dreadful name had lost its effect. Though regret for his Sister made him look upon the Prioress with abhorrence, Lorenzo could not help pitying a Woman in a situation so terrible: But in spite of all his exertions, and those of the Duke, of Don Ramirez, and the Archers, the People continued to press onwards. They forced a passage through the Guards who protected their destined Victim, dragged her from her shelter, and proceeded to take upon her a most summary and cruel vengeance. Wild with terror, and scarcely knowing what She said, the wretched Woman shrieked for a moment's mercy: She protested that She was innocent of the death of Agnes, and could clear herself from the suspicion beyond the power of doubt. The Rioters heeded nothing but the gratification of their barbarous vengeance. They refused to listen to her: They showed her every sort of insult, loaded her with mud and filth, and called her by the most opprobrious appellations. They tore her one from another, and each new Tormentor was more savage than the former. They stifled with howls and execrations her shrill cries for mercy; and dragged her through the Streets, spurning her, trampling her, and treating her with every species of cruelty which hate or vindictive fury could invent. At length a Flint, aimed by some well-directing hand, struck her full upon the temple. She sank upon the ground bathed in blood, and in a few minutes terminated her miserable existence. Yet though She no longer felt their insults, the Rioters still exercised their impotent rage upon her lifeless body. They beat it, trod upon it, and ill-used it, till it became no more than a mass of flesh, unsightly, shapeless, and disgusting.[32]

Agnes, too, is subjected to a punishment out of proportion to her crime—forced by her jealous aunt to take the veil, publicly exposed in the Church of the Capuchins, subjected to a mock death, and believing that she is about to suffer the eternal tortures of the damned, she is immured in a damp vault with only enough bread and water to keep her alive, made to bear her baby among reptiles and pestilential air, watch it die, and clutch its decaying body to her breast. Here, again, Lewis encourages a response of compassion—Agnes enunciates her heartfelt forgiveness of her tormentor—and then makes pardon nearly impossible by describing Agnes's suffering in such lurid detail:

> My slumbers were constantly interrupted by some obnoxious Insect crawling over me. Sometimes I felt the bloated Toad, hideous and pampered with the poisonous vapours of the dungeon, dragging his loathsome length along my bosom: Sometimes the quick cold Lizard rouzed me leaving his slimy track upon my face, and entangling itself in the tresses of my wild and matted hair: Often have I at waking found my fingers ringed with the long worms, which bred in the corrupted flesh of my Infant. At such times I shrieked with terror and disgust, and while I shook off the reptile, trembled with all a Woman's weakness.[33]

When Agnes is removed from her prison cell, even the sympathetic treatment accorded her by Virginia is slightly marred by the motives Lewis attributes to the young pensioner: Virginia, in love with Lorenzo, and not yet knowing the victim's identity, hopes that her attention to Agnes will 'raise her a degree in the esteem of Lorenzo'.[34] Lewis seems reluctant even to restore Agnes to perfect tranquillity: her return to happiness is expressed as a transition she must 'bear with fortitude'—'scarcely', she says, 'can my brain sustain the weight'—and she settles down to a sober marriage in full cognizance of the world's woes: 'The remaining years of Raymond and Agnes', as Lewis writes, '. . . were happy as can be those allotted to Mortals, born to be the prey of grief, and sport of disappointment.'[35]

[32] Ibid., 355–6. [33] Ibid., 415. [34] Ibid., 375. [35] Ibid., 416; 417; 420.

Even Ambrosio, at the novel's end, is refused his author's mercy: as the guards approach (as theologically they must) with his pardon, Lewis whisks him through the roof of the prison to yet greater tortures. The description of Ambrosio's fall is Lewis's most impassioned and eager passage, an escalating series of torments in which finally even the elements participate:

Headlong fell the Monk through the airy waste; The sharp point of a rock received him; and He rolled from precipice to precipice, till bruised and mangled He rested on the river's banks. Life still existed in his miserable frame: He attempted in vain to raise himself; His broken and dislocated limbs refused to perform their office, nor was He able to quit the spot where He had first fallen. The Sun now rose above the horizon; Its scorching beams darted full upon the head of the expiring Sinner. Myriads of insects were called forth by the warmth; They drank the blood which trickled from Ambrosio's wounds; He had no power to drive them from him, and they fastened upon his sores, darted their stings into his body, covered him with their multitudes, and inflicted on him tortures the most exquisite and insupportable. The Eagles of the rock tore his flesh piecemeal, and dug out his eye-balls with their crooked beaks. A burning thirst tormented him; He heard the river's murmur as it rolled beside him, but strove in vain to drag himself towards the sound. Blind, maimed, helpless, and despairing, venting his rage in blasphemy and curses, execrating his existence, yet dreading the arrival of death destined to yield him up to greater torments, six miserable days did the Villain languish. On the Seventh a violent storm arose: The winds in fury rent up rocks and forests: The sky was now black with clouds, now sheeted with fire: The rain fell in torrents: It swelled the stream; The waves overflowed their banks; They reached the spot where Ambrosio lay, and when they abated carried with them into the river the Corse of the despairing Monk.[36]

DISRUPTIONS OF TONE

The extreme trials to which Lewis exposes his characters and his often pitiless attitude towards their miseries are supplemented by a stylistic complexity that functions equally to forestall an open response to his narrative. The authorial tone of *The Monk* remains oddly detached (except, perhaps, in the

[36] Ibid., 441–2.

narration of past events (as in Raymond's story) or in the erotic sequences), whether Lewis adopts the cynical attitude of worldly wisdom of the novel's opening scene or the jubilant sadism of the Monk's downfall at the book's close. The voice that introduces the novel is sarcastic and knowing, and aggressively anti-Catholic in tone: 'Scarcely had the Abbey-Bell tolled for five minutes, and already was the Church of the Capuchins thronged with Auditors. Do not encourage the idea that the Crowd was assembled either from motives of piety or thirst of information. But very few were influenced by those reasons; and in a city where superstition reigns with such despotic sway as in Madrid, to seek for true devotion would be a fruitless attempt.'[37] In the closing sequence, Lewis's excitement is felt in his allusions to the Creation myth, and his writing gains a new solidity through the controlled biblical rhythms of his prose: '. . . six miserable days did the Villain languish. On the Seventh a violent storm arose: The winds in fury rent up rocks and forests: The sky was now black with clouds, now sheeted with fire: The rain fell in torrents; It swelled the stream; The waves overflowed their banks; They reached the spot where Ambrosio lay, and when they abated carried with them into the river the Corse of the despairing Monk.'[38] This proud use of biblical parallels (Ambrosio as Adam, experiencing his fall; Ambrosio as Satan, undergoing his expulsion from Heaven; the Decreation; the Flood) was obviously felt by Lewis to be (at least potentially) offensive, for the allusions were removed in the third edition of *The Monk* before he subjected the book to extensive bowdlerization in the fourth printing.

Further disruptions of a unified tone are created by Lewis's inclusion in (and later addition to) *The Monk* of comic characters and episodes. Such a procedure is a hallmark of the Gothic, and it has a particularly disorienting effect here, for the events of the novel are physically and psychologically more horrific than those in, for example, *The Castle of Otranto* or *The Mysteries of Udolpho*. Thus, Leonella's ridiculous behaviour with Don Christoval; the scenes in which Cunegonda is carried off, imprisoned in a closet, and eventually silenced by

[37] Ibid., 7. [38] Ibid., 442.

large draughts of cherry brandy; the long episode in which Jacintha details the arrival of Elvira's ghost spewing clouds of fire and rattling with chains grate oddly against the scenes of murder, injustice, and violation that surround them. The Gothic is by nature a mixed genre, and seems to invite such self-conscious comical retreats from tragedy: Lewis's addition (in the fourth edition of *The Monk*) of 'Giles Jollup the Grave and Brown Sally Green', a parody of his 'Alonzo the Brave, and Fair Imogine' (which he based in part on a newspaper parody of his popular ballad from *The Monk*), suggests not only his notion of the form as a sort of 'mixed grill' of prose, poetry, and miscellaneous incident, but as a receptacle for both comedy and tragedy, a genre that allows an experimental (and self-conscious) mixing of tones and incidents in the tradition of the theatrical variety show.

SUPPRESSION AND RELEASE

Given the obstacles to openness that seem built in—both formally and on the level of character—to *The Monk*, it is not surprising to find that some of the novel's most important and interesting patterns of imagery (especially sexual ones) are predicated on transference and indirection, suggesting not only Lewis's initial conservativeness in depicting sexual activity but mirroring (and again, confusingly, imitating) Ambrosio's strongly repressed sexual side. Suppression (the opposite of openness), repeatedly, is seen as a source of power in *The Monk*: its release (into knowledge) can result in unacceptable violence (as in the fall of Ambrosio) or in an effete or unhealthy refraction of energies. There are strong hints from Ambrosio's first appearance that a suppression of his sexual side directly accounts for his severity and his powers in oratory: he is presented as a striking physical figure with a 'fiery and penetrating' glance and a voice 'at once distinct and deep', a man to whom women are particularly attracted.[39] Lorenzo's description of him—'He is just at that period of life when the passions are most vigorous, unbridled, and despotic',[40] an assessment to which his dream gives additional credence—

[39] Ibid., 18; 19. [40] Ibid., 21.

signals his true nature—a nature that the Monk confirms on his return to his cell after the sermon: 'He was no sooner alone, than He gave free loose to the indulgence of his vanity. When He remembered the Enthusiasm which his discourse had excited, his heart swelled with rapture, and his imagination presented him with splendid visions of aggrandizement. He looked round him with exultation, and Pride told him loudly, that He was superior to the rest of his fellow-Creatures.'[41] The bursting forth of Ambrosio's suppressed emotions of vanity and pride is connected explicitly with his eventual sexual awakening: his language, at first an excited and frank expression of pleasure in his own power (he speaks of the 'ordeal' of youth, of subduing the violence of strong passions, of the power of his discourse), is gradually infiltrated with words with sexual connotations when he contemplates entering the outside world: 'I must now abandon the solitude of my retreat; the fairest and noblest Dames of Madrid continually present themselves at the Abbey, and will use no other Confessor. I must accustom my eyes to Objects of temptation, and expose myself to the seduction of luxury and desire. Should I meet in that world which I am constrained to enter some lovely Female, lovely . . . as you Madona. . . .!'[42] On meditating on the picture, his language and thoughts eventually become explicitly erotic: he dreams of his joy were he permitted 'to twine round my fingers those golden ringlets, and press with my lips the treasures of that snowy bosom!'[43] The mixture of the language of religious adoration and expressions of sexual ecstasy suggests the connection between Ambrosio's religious strictness and his eventual sexual incontinence: his upbringing in the convent is later described as a process of repression and narrowing, a breaking of his 'natural spirit' that perverts his good qualities into evil ones:

> For a time spare diet, frequent watching, and severe penance cooled and represt the natural warmth of his constitution: But no sooner did opportunity present itself, no sooner did He catch a glimpse of joys to which He was still a Stranger, than Religion's barriers were too feeble to resist the over-whelming torrent of his desires. All impediments yielded before the force of his temperament, warm, sanguine, and

[41] Ibid., 39–40. [42] Ibid., 40. [43] Ibid., 41.

voluptuous in the excess. As yet his other passions lay dormant; But they only needed to be once awakened, to display themselves with violence as great and irresistible.[44]

Ambrosio's repeated attempts to suppress his passionate nature result not in its annihilation but its deflection into other avenues of thought or expression. His self-rebuke ('Away, impure ideas!') after his fantasy of the Madona, though it suggests a hint of self-knowledge, is quickly covered up by heated and confused outbursts and insistences upon his own virtue, which, significantly, make use of the same vocabulary of sexual excitement: 'It is the Painter's skill that I admire, it is the Divinity that I adore! Are not the passions dead in my bosom?'[45] Outburst is succeeded by repression which produces another kind of outburst and which is quelled, interestingly, by the entrance of Rosario (who, in real life and in the Friar's emotional view, is a kind of repressed woman). The same pattern marks the episode with Agnes. Suffering under the pressures of his own thwarted sexual urges, he addresses her in terms of violent and astonishingly colourful sexual rebuke: 'Amazing confidence!', he replies to her pleas for mercy. 'What! Shall St. Clare's Convent become the retreat of Prostitutes? Shall I suffer the Church of Christ to cherish in its bosom debauchery and shame? . . . You have abandoned yourself to a Seducer's lust; You have defiled the sacred habit by your impurity . . .'[46] His initial attempts to resist temptation result in erotic dreams of seduction, frustration, and failure, and his first sight of Matilda's breast sends him rushing from the scene to his monkish cell.[47] His later attempt to repress his desire for Antonia results in the same violent action: 'worked up to phrenzy' by the scene in the magic mirror, he dashes it to the ground with the cry, 'I yield!'[48]

That such a pattern of withholding and release is erotic and violent is seen in the fates of both Ambrosio and Antonia and is implicated in the very structure of the narrative, the foreshortened episode of Ambrosio and Matilda in Volume I, Chapter II, giving way to the business-like opening of Raymond and Lorenzo in Chapter III. Some of the punish-

[44] Ibid., 237; 238–9. [45] Ibid., 41.
[46] Ibid., 46. [47] Ibid., 67; 84; 65–6. [48] Ibid., 271.

ment scenes, too, suggest the violence attendant on the sudden release of repressed energies of dislike or condemnation. In the cases of the murder of the Prioress and the public outrage against Ambrosio the author seems even to be venting a creator's rage upon his own characters.

Elvira's efforts to isolate Antonia from the real world have, unhappily, a similar effect of suppressing or stifling emotion. Her reluctance to '[remove] the bandage of ignorance [lest] the veil of innocence . . . be rent away'[49] is a pathetically misguided attempt to save her daughter from the miseries she has suffered. The result is that Antonia's *naïveté* is so acute that she is unable to interpret signals from either Lorenzo or Ambrosio; under the mistaken impression that Lorenzo's serenades are directed to another woman, and unintentionally inflaming the Monk's desires by her innocent prattle, she brings upon herself the violence that eventually annihilates her.

In the early stages of Ambrosio's corruption, the violence of released sexual energies is diverted in less direct but aesthetically more interesting ways. Scenes and images that receive the impact of transferred sexual urges mark the early part of the novel and suggest Ambrosio's (and perhaps Lewis's) reluctance to deal directly with his suppressed self. Much early or minor Gothic fiction halts at this level: unwilling to explore thoroughly the sexual emotions by which it is fascinated, it channels that curiosity into inchoate constructs of suggestive images or scenes, but never, finally, analyses them fully.

The *frisson* of a male novice transforming into a woman, who almost immediately rends open her garments to expose her breast and then resumes her anonymous habit and name, suggests perhaps deeper interests in sexuality than Lewis cared to confront. Ambrosio's attraction to Rosario, their meeting in the flowering arbour, lends a homosexual thrill to the early stages of their acquaintance: Ambrosio in a sense has already his sexual object, safely (physiologically) repressed. The scene of the centipede magnifies this pattern of complicated displacement: retrieving a rose for the (supposedly) departing Matilda/Rosario, Ambrosio is bitten (he thinks) by a serpent hidden in the bush; fainting from the 'exquisite' pain of the

[49] Ibid., 264.

wound, he sinks into Matilda/Rosario's arms.[50] The degree to which Lewis is consciously working with sexual images is debatable here: later he has Ambrosio's hand swell 'to an extraordinary size' and there are two scenes in which the swollen wound is probed with a lancet.[51] The first is withdrawn with a greenish poison, and the second with no trace of venom. When Lewis notes that Ambrosio 'struggled with desire, and shuddered when He beheld, how deep was the precipice before him',[52] he seems to be keeping even from himself the sexual connotations of his own language and scenes. Matilda's sucking of the poison, and her announcement that the poison that will cause her death once circulated in Ambrosio's veins, have a more consciously controlled effect, and Lewis will use the same image in a specifically sexual way in Ambrosio's later seduction of Matilda: 'Your veins', he cries, 'shall glow with fire, which circles in mine'.[53] The intersection of the Ambrosio–Matilda and Raymond–Agnes narratives in the early part of the novel operates on a similar principle of symbolically charged displacement: as Ambrosio sinks into Matilda's arms for his first night of guilty pleasure, Lewis embarks on a tale of extraordinary physical violence involving the plunging of daggers into husbands and sheets covered with blood.

This pattern of sexual repression and release or displacement suggests Lewis's disturbing view of sex as linked to violence, and the practice of love (or sex) as related to sadism. Indeed, Ambrosio's initial attempts to resist seduction are followed by only a brief period of uninhibited enjoyment of Matilda's charms. Resistance, once conquered in himself, shortly becomes a prerequisite to his jaded sexual urges, and force, violation (a hint possibly of the guilt and distaste he still associates with sex) become as exciting as the act of possession. His attraction to Antonia is heightened because of her distress: 'Her very tears', he notes, 'became her, and her affliction seemed to add new lustre to her charms.'[54] Later, in his cell, he thinks, 'Oh! sweeter must one kiss be snatched from the rosy lips of the First, than all the full and lustful favours bestowed so freely by the Second.'[55] Her modesty (which is conceived of as a

[50] Ibid., 71 [51] Ibid., 72; 73. [52] Ibid., 78.
[53] Ibid., 381. [54] Ibid., 241. [55] Ibid., 243.

veil (something one 'throws off'))[56] particularly arouses him, and when he approaches her bed to violate her, Lewis notes that 'there was a sort of modesty in her very nakedness, which added fresh stings to the desires of the lustful Monk'.[57] That this scene of sexual arousal results not in possession but in murder (Ambrosio's suffocation of Elvira) is the ultimate expression of the link between sex and death, and one that has been present from the novel's earliest pages. Matilda's first gesture of love to Ambrosio (the act by which she agrees to sacrifice herself for her love and the scene that initially excites him) is inextricably connected with death—she lays her dagger's point against her naked bosom—and their union is heralded by an episode that symbolically associates semen and poison (the poison from Ambrosio's wound circulating in her veins). The episode of the Bleeding Nun—herself a character of debauched and criminal lust—suggests again the violence attendant on sexuality, and the symbolic connection of sex and death by stabbing is repeated: driven by lust for her paramour's brother to murder her lover as she lies in his arms, Beatrice becomes the victim of her own sadism: the perfidious brother plunges the dagger 'still reeking with his Brother's blood in her bosom', and she expires.[58] Her haunting of Raymond—his initial confusion of her with his lover Agnes and her pressing of her cold lips to his—suggests, perhaps, as in the case of Agnes's immural in the reptile-laden dungeon, the reward for erotic pleasure: an explicit confrontation with death and decay.

This construct of sex and violence culminates in Ambrosio's encounter with Antonia in the vaults of the dead: his lust for her, once the cause of death to another (Elvira), finally becomes an expression of outright sadism and, appropriately, ends in her murder. The pattern of repression leading to violence, sex, and death is again repeated: deprived of Matilda's company, the Monk's lust has 'become madness. . . . He longed for the possession of [Antonia's] person; and even the gloom of the vault, the surrounding silence, and the resistance which He expected from her, seemed to give a fresh edge to his fierce and unbridled desires.'[59] Death and sex mix

[56] Ibid., 243. [57] Ibid., 300. [58] Ibid., 175. [59] Ibid., 380.

repeatedly: gazing on his victim, to all appearances dead through opiates and shortly to awaken to die in fact, the Monk, excited by Antonia's alarm and her 'incessant opposition', accomplishes her dishonour and then turns his hatred against himself. In the complex self-punishing speech that follows the rape, Ambrosio realizes that in violating Antonia he has accomplished his own destruction, and that his desire to possess her is connected obscurely with disgust towards himself: 'Return to your home?' he questions Antonia, '. . . That you may denounce me to the world? That you may proclaim me an Hypocrite, a Ravisher, a Betrayer, a Monster of cruelty, lust, and ingratitude? No, no, no!'[60] His murder of Antonia is the natural fulfilment of the complex: in raping Antonia, he causes her death and guarantees his eternal damnation.[61]

The repeated presence of this disturbing triangle in *The Monk* suggests, perhaps, not only the degree to which sympathy (or human love) can be perverted but the extreme difficulty of 'unmasking' or revealing certain parts of the self. The hypocrites, as Elvira constantly says of the Monk, must be unmasked,[62] yet, as Lewis more deeply knew, the process of unmasking can bring to light more volatile and dangerous emotions. Fear at such emotions may lead to repression which may result in unusual forms of transference and deflection, or in acts of violence upon the self and others. Lewis's writing in *The Monk*, in parts controlled and moralistic, in others undermining and calling into question that control by strange accesses of passion that link him to his protagonist Ambrosio, reflects the turbulence of a novelist doubting, defying, or perhaps insufficiently intrigued by his own moralistic messages of truth, candour, and mercy.

[60] Ibid., 385.

[61] See also Peter Brooks's interpretation of this scene in 'Virtue and Terror: *The Monk*', *ELH* xl (1973), 260–1.

[62] *The Monk*, pp. 263; 265.

6 Villainy: *The Italian*

The frequent disjunction of the affective and the moral in the Gothic is symptomatic of an aesthetic system with strong self-corrective tendencies, in which the affective may be used to break the bounds of the moral and the moral to repress the flights of the dramatic. In the Gothic novel, the two strains usually exist in marked tension, issuing in artistic constructs that revolve covertly or overtly around punishment, be they sentimental (as in *The Mysteries of Udolpho*) or erotic (as in *The Monk*). The peculiar fascination of the genre may reside precisely here: the reader, relieved because of his willing immersion in fantasy from contemplating the ethical implications of this struggle, can experience, under supervision, a world in which moral aberrations occur and be returned safely and confidently at the end to a domain in which such values remain properly separate. Because, furthermore, the moral tends to be applied punitively (especially at the novels' conclusions), the reader is also relieved from acting on what he has read: the works excite, in Coleridge's terms, 'feelings without at the same time ministering an impulse to action', to 'conduct according to a principle'; 'they afford excitement without producing reaction.'[1]

[1] Coleridge's remarks appear in a discussion on the education of children and are directed towards modern novels, especially ladies' novels. His sense that curiosity alone cannot stimulate moral conduct is particularly germane to the Gothic: 'The common modern novel,' he observes, 'in which there is no imagination, but a miserable struggle to excite and gratify mere curiosity, ought, in my judgment, to be wholly forbidden to children. Novel-reading of this sort is especially injurious to the growth of the imagination, the judgment, and the morals, especially to the latter, because it excites mere feelings without at the same time ministering an impulse to action. . . . The source of the common fondness for novels of this sort rests in that dislike of vacancy and that love of sloth, which are inherent in the human mind; they afford excitement without producing reaction. By reaction I mean an activity of the intellectual faculties, which shows itself in consequent reasoning and observation, and originates action and conduct according to a principle' ('The Education of Children', Lecture xi, *Literary Remains* (1836), repr. in *Coleridge's Miscellaneous Criticism*, ed. T. M. Raysor (London, 1936), pp. 195–6).

THE MORAL AND THE DRAMATIC

The difficult juggling of the moral and the dramatic in Gothic works is particularly evident in Gothic novelists' attitudes towards their villains, who propel their plots and energize the ethical systems that test the hero's and heroine's endurance. The histrionic villains of Walpole and the early Radcliffe directly uphold the moral structure of the works in which they appear because of their obvious one-dimensional badness. Walpole's Manfred flings through his castle corridors uttering the standard imprecations of villainy: 'Stop! audacious man', he cries to Father Jerome, 'and dread my displeasure'.[2] 'Rash youth, your words are air', thunders the Baron Malcolm in Radcliffe's first novel, *The Castles of Athlin and Dunbayne.*[3] Deathbed confessions and repentances on the part of such villains are nearly always devices of plot (functioning to clarify relationships or bring new facts to light), not moments in which the reader reassesses character or excuses the criminal, and the fate of evil Gothic figures is often an opportunity for vigorous moralizing: 'Their lives', Radcliffe writes in such a vein of the Marquis de Mazzini and Maria de Vellorno at the end of *A Sicilian Romance,* 'exhibited a boundless indulgence of violent and luxurious passions, and their deaths marked the consequences of such indulgence, and held forth to mankind a singular instance of divine vengeance.'[4] If such characters are to be used as exemplars (of an ethical system that has been condemned), it is of importance to the authors not to compromise their moral stands by making such villains attractive—and such restraint is normally the case in the early Gothic and the simpler examples of the genre. The villains, that is, function primarily to heighten the readers' apprehension of the unshakeable virtue of the hero and heroine.

Ambrosio and Schedoni clearly raise some questions about this framework, for both figures demand reader sym-

[2] Horace Walpole, *The Castle of Otranto: A Gothic Story,* ed. W. S. Lewis (London, 1969), p. 47.

[3] Ann Radcliffe, *The Castles of Athlin and Dunbayne. A Highland Story,* new edn. (London, 1821; repr. New York, 1972), p. 38.

[4] Ann Radcliffe, *A Sicilian Romance,* new edn. (2 vols., London, 1821; repr. 2 vols. in 1, New York, 1972), ii. 205.

pathy—either through erotic stimulation, as in *The Monk*, or, more complexly, through emotional interest, as in *The Italian*. In both instances, however, the authors retreat from a full exploration of the implications of their own creations: *The Monk* ends with a scene of retribution that effectively punishes those senses that allowed identification with Ambrosio in the first place (as the sensual gives way to the rigidly theological) and *The Italian* closes with a scene that overtly discourages a sympathetic reading of Schedoni in favour of a view of him as a species of demon, outside the human realm.

The assumption underlying such transformations (or truncations) of character is the relative unimportance of character consistency in the Gothic: much as figures (like Frederic in *The Castle of Otranto*) can be violated to allow for further complications of plot, so even in seemingly more sophisticated examples of the genre, personality is repeatedly subsumed to the demands of scenery, story, or moral. *The Italian* begins precisely with such short cuts, with the heroine and hero enacting the stereotypical roles of pining beloved and lover even when such behaviour contradicts the emotional facts: Vivaldi seeks an approbation of Ellena's affection when he has already received clear signs of it, because an evening serenade is necessary to Radcliffe's plot. In an instance that reveals such priorities more fully, St Aubert in *The Mysteries of Udolpho* is made to seem to entertain a secret passion for a woman who is not his wife, a suggestion whose ethical and emotional dimensions are utterly ignored: the 'mistake' functions not on the level of character but of story. Distinctions of character repeatedly blur (as many contemporary critics of Radcliffe's work noted) at moments of scenic importance: Ellena's fears at being abducted fade as Radcliffe enthusiastically (and meticulously) describes the sublime landscape through which she moves:

> Fainting under [the] oppression [of the heat], Ellena entreated that the windows might be open . . . and she had a glimpse of the lofty region of the mountains, but of no object that could direct her conjecture concerning where she was. She saw only pinnacles and vast precipices of various-tinted marbles, intermingled with scanty vegetation, such as stunted pinasters, dwarf oak and holly, which gave dark touches to the many-coloured cliffs, and sometimes

stretched in shadowy masses to the deep vallies, that, winding into obscurity, seemed to invite curiosity to explore the scenes beyond. Below these bold precipices extended the gloomy region of olive-trees, and lower still other rocky steeps sunk towards the plains, bearing terraces crowned with vines, and where often the artificial soil was propped by thickets of juniper, pomegranate and oleander.[5]

Such botanical observations seem as ill-timed as Ellena's exclamation at the passage's end: 'It is scarcely possible to yield to the pressure of misfortune', she cries, 'while we walk, as with the Deity, amidst his most stupendous works!'[6] Similar evidence of Radcliffe's tendency to subordinate character to mood occurs with the monk Jeronimo in the scene of Ellena and Vivaldi's escape from the monastery of San Stefano: though his gestures are repeatedly described as threatening and his voice as hollow and the old friar actually tells the lovers that they have been betrayed, his mission (it transpires later) is benign: he has no intention of hindering Ellena and Vivaldi's exodus. In this instance, atmosphere acquires an importance more pressing than consistency of character: Jeronimo is simply a device for generating temporary fear.

It is odd that a genre in which pressures of stereotype, mood, or landscape repeatedly result in odd distortions or devaluations of character has acquired the reputation of psychological complexity, for neither consistency of character (which is a prerequisite for any systematic exploration of personality) nor depth of psychological probing is characteristic of such works. When Lewis, in *The Monk*, explains (with apparent insight) that Ambrosio's natural good qualities have been perverted by convent life into narrow and selfish sentiments and his natural warmth repressed, his comments are as much a condemnation of the Church as an analysis of Ambrosio's sexually repressed state, bearing in the end more thematic and structural than pyschological precision, for the evils of the Church have been dwelt upon at length, while we have not been permitted to see the generous side of Ambrosio's personality in any systematic way. The repeated emphasis on internalization of passion in

[5] Ann Radcliffe, *The Italian or the Confessional of the Black Penitents: A Romance*, ed. F. Garber (London, 1968), p. 62.

[6] Ibid., 63.

female characters mitigates, too, against any regular investigation of the mind: endurance, not expression is the rule, an emphasis that, again, shifts attention to plot. In a slip of hand endemic to the genre, the degree to which emotions appear to be repressed may have no direct relationship to (nor may clarify) the character's inner state: as in *The Castle of Otranto* or *A Sicilian Romance*, evidence of suppression may occur without any real idea of the emotions that are supposedly at war within the character.

Indeed, one of the most intriguing paradoxes of the Gothic, as Howells has pointed out, is its tendency to emphasize emotional display, 'the outward signs of inward tensions', without any 'clear analysis of the relation between startling effects and their possible causes'.[7] This absence of specific attention to the relationship between emotional cause and effect is symptomatic of the more pervasive disjunction in the novels of the theatrical (the plot, the characters' actions) and the moral (the theme). Such a disjunction has an interesting effect on the reader of the Gothic: exposed to a series of recognizable (because usually stereotyped) signs of heightened emotional states, and discouraged from analysing them in detail, the reader enjoys the initiate's privilege of high entertainment, responding in a way that is both visceral (because excessive) and private (because apparently coded). His pleasure in reading enforces the paradox, for it depends ultimately on a depletion of meaning from the very code that encourages involvement with the work in the first place.

Such lack of cohesion between outward display and analysis is seen strikingly in Radcliffe's Schedoni who, more so than Lewis's Ambrosio, is often discussed as the prototype of the villain-hero.[8] Seemingly complex in his personality, ambiguous in his influence over his creator, Schedoni possesses a power and attractiveness that Radcliffe's earlier villains clearly lack.

[7] C. A. Howells, *Love, Mystery, and Misery: Feeling in Gothic Fiction* (London, 1978), p. 13.

[8] See, for example, Mario Praz, *The Romantic Agony,* 2nd edn., trans. A. Davidson (London, 1951), pp. 58–70. Praz argues that Byron's Giaour, Corsair, and Lara have both direct and indirect associations with Radcliffe's Schedoni. Peter L. Thorslev, jun. describes Schedoni as 'pre-Byronic'. See his discussion of the Gothic villain in *The Byronic Hero: Types and Prototypes* (Minneapolis, 1962), pp. 51–61.

Schedoni, indeed, as Scott remarked, takes over *The Italian*,[9] appropriating far more passages of description and action than Montoni or La Motte, and dominating the feeble love plot of the hero and heroine Vivaldi and Ellena. His violently internalized state, the painful evidence of remorse in his actions, and the peculiarly resonant scene in which he sits, a potential murderer, at the bedside of his supposed daughter, reveal at once his distance from the more conventionally delineated Montoni. The depth, however, of Radcliffe's investigation of Schedoni is, finally, not impressive: relegating his power over the narrative to theatrical displays of strong emotion, she creates a figure about whom, in the end, she entertains no moral uncertainties whatsoever: allowed her fascinated attention until almost the conclusion of the novel, Schedoni is at last killed off—literally and thematically—by the intrusion of a moral tone that cannot embrace the ambiguous theatricals that hint at his goodness. The suppression of Schedoni at the novel's close points not only to Radcliffe's hesitation at confronting the ethical implications of her character but to a scheme in which (as is frequent in the Gothic) the dramatic is discredited in favour of the didactic. Radcliffe's inability to explore the larger consequences of her creation suggests her limitations as a novelist of character, limitations that derive in part from the disjunction between theatrical signs and moral commentary that marks the Gothic from its inception.[10]

THEATRICALITY

From the beginning of the novel, Schedoni is invested with a role that is highly theatrical in its nature. 'His figure', Radcliffe writes, 'was striking, but not so from grace; it was tall, and, though extremely thin, his limbs were large and uncouth, and as he stalked along, wrapt in the black garments of his order,

[9] Scott calls Schedoni 'the real hero of the tale' in his 'Prefatory Memoir to Mrs Ann Radcliffe', in *The Novels of Mrs Ann Radcliffe,* Ballantyne's Novelist's Library, x (London, 1824), xii.

[10] Hugh Murray calls attention to this division in his discussion of Radcliffe: 'This writer . . . excels greatly in the representation of fierce and terrible characters; not the internal workings of these characters, but the picturesque appearance which they exhibit in the eye of the spectator' (*Morality of Fiction; or, An Inquiry into the Tendency of Fictitious Narratives, with Observations on Some of the Most Eminent* (Edinburgh, 1805)).

there was something terrible in its air; something almost superhuman.'[11] The forbidding grandeur of Schedoni's person in Apulia shocks Ellena. 'There was something . . . terrific in the silent stalk of so gigantic a form', she thinks; 'it announced both power and treachery.'[12] The superb choreography of Schedoni and Ellena's confrontation on the beach, as the Monk passes and repasses her as she tries to make her way to the fishing hamlet for protection, emphasizes his mysterious theatricality. In scenes such as these, Radcliffe's aesthetic and psychological attraction to her villain is strong: his exaggerated movements as he bends over Ellena's form suggest a genuine turmoil of soul divided between resolution and pity and Radcliffe buttresses such a reading by a detailed look into Schedoni's mind. She notes his momentary yielding to compassion under Ellena's influence and says that 'his heart seemed sensible to some touch of pity'.[13] It is chiefly Schedoni's gestures, however (his 'hasty steps', his throwing of water on Ellena's face), that encourage this interpretation, for Radcliffe has him revile himself in the melodramatic tones of villainy, and reminds us (eagerly) that '[h]e had a dagger concealed beneath his Monk's habit; as he had also an assassin's heart shrouded by his garments.'[14] In moments such as these, the tension between the moral and the dramatic view is pronounced.

Radcliffe's insistence on Schedoni's dramatic impact is seen repeatedly in the novel: she emphasizes his stature and composure again in the Inquisition scenes and invents episodes in which he figures as a central picturesque element. As the Marchesa passes by a window in one such scene, the evening gleam falls suddenly on Schedoni's face and she starts at his expression.[15] When Vivaldi and the Marchese enter Schedoni's cell at the end of the novel, feeble light coming through the dungeon grate shows a countenance shrunken and ghastly, one from which Vivaldi averts his face.[16] The irony of this emphasis on expressive gesture, however, is that, like many of the signs in *The Italian,* the surface appearance does not always reveal the truth. Such a fact calls into question a central premise of Gothic coding, for the countenance and air of a character

[11] *The Italian,* pp. 34–5. [12] Ibid., 221. [13] Ibid., 223. [14] Ibid., 224. [15] Ibid., 175. [16] Ibid., 389–90.

usually have a direct relationship to his or her moral state. Ellena and Olivia, thus, not only announce their virtue by their appearance and behaviour, but recognize (on one level) their consanguinity through how they look. When Ellena is attracted by Olivia's melancholy and expressive voice in the convent and moments later sees her face, she discovers 'a countenance, that instantly confirmed her conjecture',[17] and Olivia, similarly, seems instinctively and immediately to recognize her daughter: Radcliffe notes that she seems 'unwilling to withdraw her eyes from Ellena'.[18]

Schedoni exhibits a face that alternates from relaying little information to reflecting directly the condition of his soul. His ability to 'adapt himself to the tempers and passions of persons, whom he wished to conciliate'[19] is guaranteed by an expressive vocabulary that varies from meekness and holiness[20] to severity and craft,[21] and he seems able to assume such expressions at will. This emphasis on Schedoni's chameleon-like nature (at one point in the novel he is described specifically as reptilian)[22] marks him instantly as a villain: his penchant for assuming disguises links him to Satan and divides him from all Radcliffe's virtuous characters whose minds find innocent expression in the face.

DEPRIVATIONS AND CONFUSIONS OF MEANING

Schedoni's most powerful art, however, lies not in his theatrical posing but in his internalization of passion, his ability to remain expressionless and silent in situations that threaten to expose him. Repeatedly in the novel, he adopts an air of abstraction, of inwardness that conveys nothing of his true state. As Vivaldi eagerly watches his countenance for signs of alarm as

[17] Ibid., 86.

[18] Ibid., 87. This is a pattern that, as Eve Kosofsky Sedgwick has pointed out, characterizes the Gothic. See 'The Character in the Veil: Imagery of the Surface in the Gothic Novel', *PMLA* xcvi (1981), 255–70. Sophia Lee's *The Recess* (a novel Sedgwick does not discuss) revolves repeatedly around questions of familial relationships posed by portraits.

[19] *The Italian*, p. 35.

[20] Ibid., 35; 53; 169; 170.

[21] Ibid., 48.

[22] Ibid.,171.

he accuses him of frequenting Paluzzi, it suffers no change.[23] In the masterful scene in the church of the Spirito Santo, Vivaldi rants and gesticulates at Schedoni as the Confessor stands motionless, his features fixed and his eyes bent to the ground.[24] He adopts the same solemn and mysterious stance at his interrogation and, when the sentence of his trial is pronounced, remains expressionless. Schedoni's power to suppress emotion is seen strikingly in scenes in which his countenance shifts (voluntarily or involuntarily) from expressive to rigid: accused by Vivaldi of poisoning the repose of his family, he unexpectedly changes expression: 'A dark malignity overspread the features of the monk, and at that moment Vivaldi thought he beheld a man, whose passions might impel him to the perpetration of almost any crime, how hideous soever. He recoiled from him, as if he had suddenly seen a serpent in his path, and stood gazing on his face, with an attention so wholly occupied as to be unconscious that he did so. Schedoni almost instantly recovered himself . . .'[25] When Schedoni grasps Ellena's arm on the beach, his visage becomes 'so terrible' that Ellena struggles to free herself, but when she looks at him, his eyes have 'assumed the fixt and vacant glare of a man, whose thoughts have retired within themselves, and who is no longer conscious to surrounding objects'.[26]

Schedoni's refusal to externalize his emotions is in keeping with a book that gathers impact from 'hieroglyphics' of doubtful import.[27] The characters of *The Italian* come repeatedly upon signs whose meanings are threatening yet unclear: the heap of bloody garments in Paluzzi, the mattress of straw in the cave where Vivaldi and Ellena are led by Jeronimo, the bloody dagger that Nicola presents to Vivaldi and then to Schedoni at the Inquisition. Schedoni's room, fittingly, epitomizes such suggestive deprivations of meaning: 'The chamber', Vivaldi observes, 'contained little more than a mattress, a chair, a table, and a crucifix; some books of devotion were upon the table, one or two of which were written in unknown characters; several instruments of torture lay beside them.'[28] Schedoni's room is an architectural rendition of his face: spare, evocative,

[23] Ibid., 50. [24] Ibid., 103–5. [25] Ibid., 51.
[26] Ibid., 222. [27] Ibid., 140. [28] Ibid., 102.

unexplained. Its 'print of truth' (to use Nicola's words as he points dramatically to the blade of the poniard in Vivaldi's cell) is both clear and unclear: obvious in its importance yet obscure, finally, in its meaning.

The reader's compulsion to invest such signs with meaning is mirrored not only in Vivaldi's tormented questioning of and about Schedoni at the beginning and end of the novel but in the trick of the miniature which, stunningly, both is and is not Schedoni. Here, external evidence (the portrait), in confirming Schedoni's identity, falsifies a deeper truth: though the portrait is of Schedoni, it is not of Ellena's father. Such a logical construct (in which the falsity of one premise (Ellena's) must lead to a wrong conclusion (Schedoni = Ellena's father)) shows the errors of identity that both expand Schedoni's character and locate him at the centre of a semiotic system that is based on false extensions of meaning. The masterful play on the word 'father' (which Ellena utters as she awakens to find Schedoni at her bed) epitomizes this confusion, for while Ellena addresses Schedoni in his religious capacity, Schedoni 'hears' the paternal meaning. The false homonym is lent further resonance by Olivia's early (rightful) appellations of Ellena as her 'child' and 'daughter'.[29]

Much as Schedoni's power is augmented by what he does not reveal, so he gains impact through his confusion with Nicola (who frequents the ruins of Paluzzi) and Spalatro (whose villainy is a direct reflection of Schedoni's criminal past). Such expansions of character occur throughout the book. Schedoni's story is retailed many times without explicitly naming him and, though the comparison must be performed retroactively, he also bears an unmistakable resemblance to the assassin who arrests the English travellers' attention in the novel's opening pages and whose entrance into the confessional causes the Italian to recall his story. Not only has this mysterious figure found shelter in the same church (and confessional) in which Schedoni admitted his crime; he assumes the familiar posture of the monk: tall and thin, habited in a cloak that 'muffle[s] the lower part of his countenance', he stands with his arms folded and his 'eyes directed towards the ground'.[30] Schedoni, in fact,

[29] Ibid., 127; 126. [30] Ibid., 1.

is brought to mind by nearly every other mysterious figure of evil in the book (as, for example, the 'gigantic figure' of the man who interrupts Vivaldi and Ellena's marriage, and the Barône di Cambrusca, whose story of crime is actually Schedoni's). Such a proliferation of Schedoni-like figures suggests not only that Schedoni displays characteristics that Radcliffe viewed as archetypically criminal; it reveals that Schedoni has, on a structural level, taken over the narrative, for all criminals are versions of him or recall him. In the case of Nicola, in particular, whose identity is not revealed until the novel's close, the confusion with Schedoni is systematically encouraged by Radcliffe's insistence on his thrilling voice, his mysterious comportment in the ruins, and his threatening messages to Vivaldi, as well as by Vivaldi's speculations about the identity of his persecutor:

> . . . as he listened to the deep tones of Schedoni's voice, he became almost certain, that they were not the accents of his unknown adviser, though he considered, at the same moment, that it was not difficult to disguise, or to feign a voice. His stature seemed to decide the question more reasonably; for the figure of Schedoni appeared taller than that of the stranger; and though there was something of resemblance in their air, which Vivaldi had never observed before, he again considered, that the habit of the same order, which each wore, might easily occasion an artificial resemblance.[31]

In such passages, Radcliffe pursues the labyrinthine logic that marks her dealings with Schedoni throughout the book: his character is assessed through a procedure of negative proofs, a confused discarding of outward signs in favour of an internal truth that those signs more often than not contradict. Such a pattern, indeed, characterizes Schedoni from his first description in the novel: what is not known of him (his family, his attitude towards religion) is taken by some members of his order for as compelling a proof of his guilt as the emotion that no longer invigorates his face. His physiognomy, Radcliffe writes, 'bore the traces of many passions, which seemed to have fixed the features they no longer animated'.[32] Schedoni's face at once reveals his past and prohibits interpretation of his present

[31] Ibid., 49. [32] Ibid., 35.

state: it is the ultimate mask, telling simultaneously all and nothing. When Schedoni is identified as Ellena's father, fact and inner truth seem temporarily to coincide: the reader's sympathy with him is encouraged not only through his (apparent) relationship to the heroine but through the tears Radcliffe shows him shedding at Ellena's bedside. Radcliffe's repeated shifting of point of view to Schedoni (in this and other scenes) encourages an identification with her villain that she approaches elsewhere only with La Motte, and she implicitly urges us to a sympathetic treatment of him in Vivaldi's hesitation to judge him before and during the trial.

MORAL STABILIZING

The complex moral response demanded of the reader when Schedoni, approaching Ellena's bed to murder her, at the next moment sinks to her side and weeps, or when he instinctively breaks through his reserve during Ansaldo's testimony to question the priest about Olivia's virtue is not, however, maintained by Radcliffe to the novel's end. Indeed, as if in fear of what she has created, Radcliffe steps in with a punitive moral tone and erases many of the complexities we have associated with Schedoni. The result is (as with La Motte) a kind of death by authorial (and moral) fiat: an abandoning of mixed sympathy in favour of a system that delineates moral options with comforting clarity.

Such protective gestures have occurred throughout the novel: Schedoni is often called explicitly 'crafty' and 'severe', 'cunning', 'ferocious', and 'terrible' (though such terms may be used in a positive theatrical sense as much as in a moral one), and Radcliffe has not hesitated overtly to condemn his hypocrisy. The epigraphs of the chapters, too, repeatedly point to his villainy. As if in imitation of Lewis (or Shakespeare), Radcliffe insists pre-emptively that 'ambition' has motivated Schedoni's crimes: he desires, we are told, a high office in the church. and such a rationale recurs more frequently towards the novel's close. Aside from what we know of Schedoni's haughty disposition, such a motivation (as in the case of Iago) fails to convince. Schedoni's willingness to involve himself in the Marchesa's plot seems to derive from some much deeper cause (which his theatrical gestures suggest)—one rooted in self-hatred (which the instruments of torture in his room imply), disgust towards the world, and a nihilistic propensity to destruction.

The author's moral rejection (and simplification) of Schedoni grows more pronounced towards the story's end: as he and Ellena draw near Naples, the narrative voice delivers increasingly lengthy condemnations of his behaviour,[33] and the rise of Olivia (the true parent) in the last chapters of the novel necessarily results in a demotion of Schedoni—in part because of Olivia's exemplary virtue and because the two characters are radically opposed as a result of Schedoni's original crime. Indeed, the figures are explicitly contrasted after the reunion of Ellena and her mother: 'It may be worthy of observation,' Radcliffe remarks, 'that the virtues of Olivia, exerted in a general cause, had thus led her unconsciously to the happiness of saving her daughter; while the vices of Schedoni had as unconsciously urged him nearly to destroy his niece . . .'[34]

Indeed, the complex emphasis on psychology which has periodically deepened Schedoni's character collapses in the final third of the novel into questions of identity as the reader struggles (along with Vivaldi) to trace Schedoni's past and determine his true relationship to Ellena, Spalatro, and Nicola. The interrogation and trial in the chambers of the Inquisition become, in effect, an analogue for the reader's disposition towards the novel at the end: fact-finding, an emphasis on past actions, replaces those subtle (if inchoate) explorations of Schedoni's remorse and his goodness. The last part of the book thus fragments into a series of hurried narratives designed to reveal the truth: Ansaldo's account of the confession, Spalatro's deathbed demand for revenge, Nicola's testimony. Thrown back into Schedoni's criminal past, our apprehension of his compassion and suffering fades and, in the end, Radcliffe imposes on him a deed that estranges our sympathy from him for good: he commits an act of murder and suicide that brands him as inhuman. The horror of the company compelled to witness his dissolution and the death of Nicola is marked, and Radcliffe underlines the animalistic (or

[33] Ibid., 289. [34] Ibid., 384.

unearthly) side of Schedoni in his cry of exultation at Nicola's death: 'At the instant of [Nicola's] fall, Schedoni uttered a sound so strange and horrible, so convulsed, yet so loud, so exulting, yet so unlike any human voice, that every person in the chamber, except those who were assisting Nicola, struck with irresistible terror, endeavoured to make their way out of it.'[35] The yell is called 'demoniacal' and the mystery of how the poison was conveyed past the guards of the Inquisition and to Nicola remains unsolved: as so often in life, Schedoni refuses to answer the question and dies without satisfying the inquisitor's demand. Schedoni's death is evocative because it is, in part, his grandest theatrical gesture, but even in this most expressive act the threat of the unexpressed and unexplained is explicit. The moral condemnation under which he dies (the hint that he is, finally, more demon than man) threatens in yet another way to extinguish his complexity as both character and villain. A similar pattern closes the novel as, with dancing and shouting, the nuptials of Vivaldi and Ellena are celebrated in 'a scene of fairy-land' that leaves all memory of the Inquisition behind.[36] Paulo's shouts of '*O! giorno felíce! O! giorno felíce!*' in effect drown out those deeper, darker tones that characterized the earlier sections of the novel, and the reader is transported into a world in which moral values and familial relationships, once skewed, are set happily to rights (though in doing so, Radcliffe pays tribute to a moral and emotional system that lies outside her own novel). Schedoni's power may linger, but it is clearly not meant to; rather, our attitude towards him ought, ideally, to approximate Ellena's when she learns of the closeness of their relationship: we should suspect his real motives and find his approach to paternal tenderness (and our own sympathy) the most frightening of all.

[35] Ibid., 402. [36] Ibid., 412.

Epilogue

A successful response to the Gothic is based on instability: one must be pleased by what one dreads, take pleasure from distress, luxuriate in terror. Though this paradox was repeatedly noted by critics of the period, and recurs in discussions of the sublime, it poses problems for the reader of Gothic fiction that are particularly disquieting. It is perhaps the peculiarly contradictory stance of the reader of Gothic that accounts for the emphasis on decay and disintegration in the form. Because the Gothic, though it retains its outward moral structure, increasingly flirts with ambivalence in ethics (the ascendancy of Schedoni in *The Italian,* the Gothic heroes of Lewis and Maturin, the works of William Godwin), the position of an audience that abandons itself to such pleasures without the witting supervision of an author or the reward of controlled moral truths becomes equivocal at best. That the search for disquieting effects could become amoral was a consequence realized by the earliest theoreticians of the picturesque;[1] that the amoral or immoral itself could become fascinating was a premise explored by the later practitioners of the Gothic. As one approaches this latter pole, the delicate instability of balance that ideally defines the Gothic becomes more fixed: one's imagination cannot, as Ann Radcliffe hopefully argued, be infinitely 'expanded' by terror,[2] but is inevitably periodically stupefied and fixed by it. The fixation exercised by evil and horror in the narratives of Godwin or Maturin is, indeed, petrifying and numbing; Emily's response when Morano enters her bedroom, or when she views what she thinks is the corpse of Madame Montoni, is equally dangerously debilitating. Thus, the most dramatic and striking scenes of Gothic death are fixed like pictures (Everhard covered with blood in *Melmoth the Wanderer;* the flayed novitiate in *Melmoth;* the burial of Madame Montoni in *The Mysteries of*

[1] Knight and Gilpin, among others, make frequent reference to this problem.

[2] Ann Radcliffe, 'On the Supernatural in Poetry', *New Monthly Magazine,* xvi (1826), 149.

Udolpho); they freeze the soul and defy a constructive response. The paradox of the Gothic is that the genre, despite its close connection to sentimental narrative, actually prohibits sentimental and dynamic judgements on the part of its readers: by exhibiting such extreme emotion in others, it denies that opportunity to its audience. Part of the problem lies, as Scott detected, in the tendency of its writers to aggravate and overwork a sensation that is essentially fragile. '[T]he finest and deepest feelings', he wrote in his review of Maturin's *Fatal Revenge*, 'are those which are most easily exhausted. The cord which vibrates and sounds at a touch, remains in silent tension under continued pressure.'[3] Scott's realization of this problem is crucial to an understanding of where the Gothic fails: 'It is said,' he continues, 'respecting the cruel punishment of breaking alive upon the wheel, the sufferer's nerves are so much jarred by the first blow, that he feels comparatively little pain from those which follow. There is something of this in moral feeling; nor do we see a better remedy for it than to recommend the cessation of these experiments upon the public, until their sensibility shall have recovered its original tone.'[4] The Gothic, indeed, seems to gain its most characteristic effects through a complex procedure of deprivation and destruction; tantalizing its audience with emotions that it cannot fully feel, it manufactures, as Coleridge detected in reading the work of Ann Radcliffe, an atmosphere approaching moral eroticism. 'Curiosity', he observed, 'is raised oftener than it is gratified; or rather, it is raised so high that no adequate gratification can be given it; the interest is completely dissolved when once the adventure is finished, and the reader, when he is got to the end of the work, looks about in vain for the spell which had bound him so strongly to it.'[5]

That sensitivity can through repeated exposure be converted to callousness is one of the most troubling moral paradoxes of the Gothic. Our reaction to the terrible is perhaps closest to

[3] [Sir Walter Scott], Review of *Fatal Revenge*, in the *Quarterly Review*, iii (1810), 346.

[4] Ibid., 346.

[5] [Coleridge], Review of *The Mysteries of Udolpho*, in the *Critical Review*, 2nd ser., xi (1794), 362; repr. in *Coleridge's Miscellaneous Criticism*, ed. T. M. Raysor (London, 1936), p. 357.

that voiced by the parricide in *Melmoth the Wanderer* as he watches the decay of the lovers at the door of their underground prison: 'We glory in our impenetrability'. 'If you suffer', as the parricide later puts it, 'I am saved.'[6] Monçada on his tower, fascinated by the scene of mob violence; Emily fixing her eager gaze on the corpse of Madame Montoni; the repeated illustrations in Gothic novels of fainting maidens;[7] and the pictorial freezes with which the genre abounds are all analogues to the reader's response to the Gothic: allured and then stupefied by an excess of horror, he cannot, finally, entertain the complex response of ambivalence that the form ideally demands. It is not, as in the figure of the classical Greek Gorgon, the mixture of beauty and horror that petrifies, but the exhaustion at being tantalized by meaning and finally being denied it that is so vexing.[8] The complex combination of the superficial and the conventionally significant that impel the reader outward and the forays into the darker territory of moral ambivalence of the later Gothic, if it stabilizes, does so at last only with difficulty—in aesthetic failure, as in Shelley's *St. Irvyne* or in the superficial shock of horror-Gothic.

[6] Charles Robert Maturin, *Melmoth the Wanderer: A Tale*, ed. D. Grant (London, 1968), pp. 207; 225.

[7] See Maurice Lévy's catalogue of illustrations in Gothic fiction, *Images du roman noir* (Paris, 1973).

[8] As an anonymous reviewer of Lewis's *Feudal Tyrants* noted with weariness in *The Critical Review*, 3rd ser., xi (1807), 274: '[G]hosts, bones, chains, dungeons, castles, forests, murders, and rapine pass before us in long order, till sated with horrors and habituated to their view we regard them with as much composure as an undertaker contemplates the last melancholy rites of his mortal brethren.'

Bibliography

'A Jacobin Novelist' [Letter to the editor], in the *Monthly Magazine,* iv (1798), 102–4.

The Age; A Poem: Moral, Political, and Metaphysical. With Illustrative Annotations. In Ten Books (London, 1810).

Alexander, B. (ed.), *Life at Fonthill, 1807–1822* (London, 1957).

Altick, R. D., *The English Common Reader: A Social History of the Mass Reading Public, 1800–1900* (Chicago, 1957).

Ames, D. S., 'Strawberry Hill: Architecture of the "as if" ', in R. Runte (ed.), *Studies in Eighteenth-century Culture,* viii (Madison, 1979), 351–63.

Andrews, Miles Peter, *The Mysteries of the Castle: A Dramatic Tale, in Three Acts* (London, 1795).

'Anti Ghost', 'On the New Method of Inculcating Morality' [Letter to the editor], in *Walker's Hibernian Magazine; or, Compendium of Entertaining Knowledge* (1798), pt. i, pp. 10–12.

Austen, Jane, *Northanger Abbey,* ed. J. Davie (London, 1971).

Barrett, Eaton Stannard, *The Heroine, or Adventures of Cherubina,* 2nd edn. (3 vols., London, 1814).

Bayer-Berenbaum, L., *The Gothic Imagination: Expansion in Gothic Literature and Art* (Rutherford, NJ, 1982).

Beckford, William, *Dreams, Waking Thoughts and Incidents,* ed. R. J. Gemmett (Rutherford, NJ, 1971).

—— *Modern Novel Writing* (1796) and *Azemia* (1797), with an introd. by H. M. Levy, jun. (4 vols. repr. in 1 vol., Gainesville, 1970).

—— *The Travel-Diaries of William Beckford of Fonthill,* ed. G. Chapman (2 vols., Cambridge, 1928).

—— *Vathek,* ed. R. Lonsdale (London, 1970).

Birkhead, E., *The Tale of Terror: A Study of the Gothic Romance* (London, 1921; repr. New York, 1963).

Blakey, D., *The Minerva Press 1790–1820* (Printed for the Bibliographical Society at the University Press, Oxford, 1939 (for 1935)).

Brauchli, J., *Der englische Schauerroman um 1800 unter Berücksichtigung der unbekannten Bücher: Ein Beitrag zur Geschichte der Volksliteratur* (Weida i. Thür., 1928).

Bredvold, L. I., *The Natural History of Sensibility* (Detroit, 1962).

Breton, A., *Les Vases communicants* (Paris, 1955).

—— 'Limites non frontières du surréalisme', *Nouvelle revue française,* xlviii (1937), 200–15.

Brooks, P., *The Melodramatic Imagination: Balzac, Henry James, Melodrama, and the Mode of Excess* (New Haven, 1976).

Brooks, P., 'Virtue and Terror: *The Monk*', *ELH* xl (1973), 249–63.

Burke, Edmund, *A Philosophical Enquiry into the Origin of Our Ideas of the Sublime and Beautiful,* ed. J. T. Boulton (London, 1958).

Byrd, M., 'The Madhouse, the Whorehouse, and the Convent', *Partisan Review,* xliv (1977), 268–78.

Catalogue of The Third Portion of the Beckford Library, Removed from Hamilton Palace (London, 1883).

Chew, S., 'The Nineteenth Century and After (1789–1939)', in A. C. Baugh (ed.), *A Literary History of England* (New York, 1948), pp. 1109–605.

Clark, K., *The Gothic Revival: An Essay in the History of Taste,* rev. edn. (New York, 1962).

[Coleridge, Samuel Taylor], Review of M. G. Lewis, *The Monk,* in the *Critical Review,* 2nd ser., xix (1797), 194–200; repr. in *Coleridge's Miscellaneous Criticism,* ed. T. M. Raysor (London, 1936), pp. 370–8.

—— Review of Ann Radcliffe, *The Mysteries of Udolpho,* in the *Critical Review,* 2nd ser., xi (1794), 361–72; repr. in *Coleridge's Miscellaneous Criticism,* ed. T. M. Raysor (London, 1936), pp. 355–70.

—— 'The Education of Children', Lecture xi, *Literary Remains* (1836), repr. in *Coleridge's Miscellaneous Criticism,* ed. T. M. Raysor (London, 1936), pp. 194–6.

Cottom, D., *The Civilized Imagination: A Study of Ann Radcliffe, Jane Austen, and Sir Walter Scott* (Cambridge, 1985).

Dacre, Charlotte, *Zofloya; or, The Moor: A Romance of the Fifteenth Century* (3 vols., London, 1806; repr. New York, 1974).

Daiches, D., *A Critical History of English Literature* (2 vols., London, 1960).

Day, W. P., *In the Circles of Fear and Desire: A Study of Gothic Fantasy* (Chicago, 1985).

Doody, M. A., 'Deserts, Ruins and Troubled Waters: Female Dreams in Fiction and the Development of the Gothic Novel', *Genre,* x (1977), 529–72.

Dunlop, J. C., *History of Prose Fiction,* rev. edn. (2 vols., London, 1888), ed. H. Wilson.

Durant, D., 'Ann Radcliffe and the Conservative Gothic', *Studies in English Literature,* xxii (1982), 519–30.

Ehlers, L. A., 'The Gothic World as Stage: Providence and Character in *The Castle of Otranto*', *Wascana Review,* xiv. ii (1979), 17–30.

[Enfield, W.], Review of *The Mysteries of Udolpho*, in the *Monthly Review*, 2nd ser., xv (1794), 278–83.

Evans, B., *Gothic Drama from Walpole to Shelley*, University of California Publications in English, xviii (Berkeley and Los Angeles, 1947).

Evelyn, John, 'An Account of Architects and Architecture, Together, With an Historical, Etymological Explanation of certain Terms, particularly Affected by Architects', enlarged and improved, in R. Fréart, *A Parallel of the Antient Architecture with the Modern*, 2nd edn. (London, 1707).

Fiedler, L. A., *Love and Death in the American Novel*, rev. edn. (New York, 1966).

Foster, J. R., 'The Abbé Prevost and the English Novel', *PMLA* xlii (1927), 443–64.

—— *History of the Pre-romantic Novel in England*, Modern Language Association Monograph Series, xvii (New York, 1949).

Foucault, M., *Madness and Civilization: A History of Insanity in the Age of Reason*, trans. R. Howard (London, 1967).

Freud, Sigmund, 'The "Uncanny" ' (1919), in *The Standard Edition of the Complete Psychological Works of Sigmund Freud*, ed. and trans. J. Strachey *et al.*, xvii (London, 1955), 217–56.

Garber, F., 'Meaning and Mode in Gothic Fiction', in H. E. Pagliaro (ed.), *Studies in Eighteenth-century Culture*, iii. *Racism in the Eighteenth Century* (Cleveland, 1973), 155–69.

Gilbert, S. M., and S. Gubar, *The Madwoman in the Attic: The Woman Writer and the Nineteenth-century Literary Imagination* (New Haven, 1979).

Gilpin, William, *Observations on the River Wye, and Several Parts of South Wales, &c. Relative Chiefly to Picturesque Beauty; Made in the Summer of the Year 1770*, 2nd edn. (London, 1789).

—— *Observations on the Western Parts of England, Relative Chiefly to Picturesque Beauty. To Which Are Added, A Few Remarks on the Picturesque Beauties of the Isle of Wight* (London, 1798).

—— *Observations, Relative Chiefly to Picturesque Beauty, Made in the Year 1772, On Several Parts of England; Particularly the Mountains, and Lakes of Cumberland, and Westmoreland* (2 vols., London, 1786).

—— *Observations, Relative Chiefly to Picturesque Beauty, Made in the Year 1776, On Several Parts of Great Britain; Particularly the High-Lands of Scotland* (2 vols., London, 1789).

—— *Remarks on Forest Scenery, and Other Woodland Views, (Relative Chiefly to Picturesque Beauty) Illustrated by the Scenes of New-Forest in Hampshire. In Three Books* (2 vols., London, 1791).

'The Gothic Story of the Castle of Otranto', in the *Universal Magazine,* xxxvi (1765), 202–8; 235–42.

Graham, K. W., 'Implications of the Grotesque: Beckford's *Vathek* and the Boundaries of Fictional Reality', *Tennessee Studies in Literature,* xxiii (1978), 61–74.

[Graves, Richard], *Plexippus: or, The Aspiring Plebeian* (2 vols., London, 1790).

Haggerty, G. E., 'Fact and Fancy in the Gothic Novel', *Nineteenth-century Fiction,* xxxix (1985), 379–91.

Hart, F. R., 'Limits of the Gothic: The Scottish Example', in H. E. Pagliaro (ed.), *Studies in Eighteenth-century Culture,* iii. *Racism in the Eighteenth Century* (Cleveland, 1973), 137–53.

Hazlitt, William, *The Complete Works of William Hazlitt,* ed. P. P. Howe (21 vols., London, 1930–4).

Hogle, J. E., 'The Restless Labyrinth: Cryptonymy in the Gothic Novel', *Arizona Quarterly,* xxxvi (1980), 330–58.

Holland, N. N., and L. F. Sherman, 'Gothic Possibilities', *New Literary History,* viii (1977), 279–94.

Howells, C. A., *Love, Mystery, and Misery: Feeling in Gothic Fiction* (London, 1978).

Hume, R. D., 'Gothic Versus Romantic: A Revaluation of the Gothic Novel', *PMLA* lxxxiv (1969), 282–90.

Hurd, Richard, *Letters on Chivalry and Romance, with the Third Elizabethan Dialogue,* ed. and with an introd. by E. J. Morley (London, 1911).

Isabelle et Théodore (Paris, 1797).

Jephson, Robert, *The Count of Narbonne: A Tragedy* (London, 1781); repr. in *The Plays of Robert Jephson,* ed. T. J. Maynard (New York, 1980).

Kant, Immanuel, *The Critique of Judgement,* trans. J. C. Meredith (Oxford, 1952).

Kaufman, P., *The Community Library: A Chapter in English Social History,* Transactions of the American Philosophical Society, NS lvii. vii (1967).

—— 'In Defense of Fair Readers', *Review of English Literature,* viii (1967), 68–76.

Kelly, G., ' "A Constant Vicissitude of Interesting Passions": Ann Radcliffe's Perplexed Narratives', *Ariel,* x (1979), 45–64.

—— *The English Jacobin Novel 1780–1805* (Oxford, 1976).

Kiely, R., *The Romantic Novel in England* (Cambridge, Mass., 1972).

Killen, A. M., *Le Roman terrifiant ou roman noir de Walpole à Anne Radcliffe et son influence sur la littérature française jusqu'en 1840* (Paris, 1923).

Leavis, Q. D., *Fiction and the Reading Public* (London, 1932).

Lee, Sophia, *The Recess; or, A Tale of Other Times* (3 vols., London, 1783–5; repr. New York, 1972).

—— and Harriet Lee, *The Canterbury Tales,* rev. and corr. (2 vols., London, 1832; repr. New York, 1978).

Leland, Thomas, *Longsword, Earl of Salisbury: An Historical Romance,* ed. J. C. Stephens, jun. (New York, 1957).

Lévy, M., *Images du roman noir* (Paris, 1973).

—— *Le Roman 'gothique' anglais 1764–1824,* Publications de la Faculté des Lettres et Sciences Humaines de Toulouse, sér. A, t. 9 (Toulouse, 1968).

Lewis, Matthew (M. G.), *Le Moine* (4 vols., Paris, 1798).

—— *The Monk: A Romance* (3 vols., Paris, 1807).

—— *The Monk: A Romance,* ed. H. Anderson (London, 1973).

Lewis, P., 'Fearful Lessons: The Didacticism of the Early Gothic Novel', *College Language Association Journal,* xxiii (1980), 470–84.

Lewis, W. S., 'The Genesis of Strawberry Hill', *Metropolitan Museum Studies,* v.i (1934), 57–92.

Lovejoy, A. O., 'The First Gothic Revival and the Return to Nature', *Modern Language Notes,* xxvii (1932), 414–46.

MacAndrew, E., *The Gothic Tradition in Fiction* (New York, 1979).

Macaulay, Thomas Babington, Review of *Letters of Horace Walpole . . . to Sir Horace Mann,* in the *Edinburgh Review,* lviii (1833), 227–58.

McFarland, T., *Romanticism and the Forms of Ruin: Wordsworth, Coleridge, and Modalities of Fragmentation* (Princeton, NJ, 1981).

McIntyre, C. F., *Ann Radcliffe in Relation to Her Time* (New Haven, 1920; repr. London, 1970).

—— 'The Later Career of the Elizabethan Villain-Hero', *PMLA* xl (1925), 874–80.

—— 'Were the "Gothic Novels" Gothic?', *PMLA* xxxvi (1921), 644–67.

McKillop, A. D., 'Mrs. Radcliffe on the Supernatural in Poetry', *JEGP* xxxi (1932), 352–9.

—— 'On the Acquisition of Minor English Fiction 1740–1800', *Newberry Library Bulletin,* 2nd ser., iv (1956), 70–4.

[Mathias, T. J.], *The Pursuits of Literature: A Satirical Poem in Four Dialogues. With Notes,* new edn., rev. and corr. (London, 1797).

Maturin, Charles Robert, *Fatal Revenge; or, The Family of Montorio. A Romance* (3 vols., London, 1807).

—— *Melmoth the Wanderer: A Tale,* ed. D. Grant (London, 1968).

Maturin, Charles Robert, *The Milesian Chief. A Romance* (4 vols. in 2, London, 1812; repr. 4 vols., New York, 1979).

May, L. C., *Parodies of the Gothic Novel* (New York, 1980).

Mayo, R. D., *The English Novel in the Magazines (1740–1815)* (Evanston, 1962).

— 'Gothic Romance in the Magazines', *PMLA* lxv (1950), 762–89.

— 'The Gothic Short Story in the Magazines', *Modern Language Review,* xxxvii (1942), 448–54.

— 'How Long Was Gothic Fiction in Vogue?' *Modern Language Notes,* lviii (1943), 58–64.

Meek, Mrs. [Mary Meeke], *Count St. Blancard, or, The Prejudiced Judge, A Novel* (3 vols., London, 1795).

Miyoshi, M. *The Divided Self: A Perspective on the Literature of the Victorians* (New York, 1969).

'Modern Literature', *Aberdeen Magazine: or, Universal Repository,* iii (1798), 338–40.

Moers, E., *Literary Women* (New York, 1976).

Monk, S. H., *The Sublime: A Study of Critical Theories in XVIII-century England* (Ann Arbor, 1960).

Morris, D. B., 'Gothic Sublimity', *New Literary History,* xvi (1985), 299–319.

Murphy, Dennis Jasper, see Charles Robert Maturin.

Murray, H., *Morality of Fiction; or, An Inquiry into the Tendency of Fictitious Narratives, with Observations on Some of the Most Eminent* (Edinburgh, 1805).

Nelson, L., jun., 'Night Thoughts on the Gothic Novel', *Yale Review,* lii (1962), 236–57.

Norton, R., 'Aesthetic Gothic Horror', *Yearbook of Comparative and General Literature,* no. 21 (1972), pp. 31–40.

Parreaux, A., *The Publication of 'The Monk': A Literary Event 1796–1798* (Paris, 1960).

Parsons, Eliza, *Castle of Wolfenbach* (London, 1793; repr. London, 1968).

Paulson, R., *Representations of Revolution (1789–1820)* (New Haven, 1983).

Pinkerton, J., *Walpoliana* (2 vols., London, 1799).

Platzner, R. L., and R. D. Hume, ' "Gothic Versus Romantic": A Rejoinder', *PMLA* lxxxvi (1971), 266–74.

Poovey, M., 'Ideology and *The Mysteries of Udolpho', Criticism,* xxi (1979), 307–30.

Porte, J., 'In the Hands of an Angry God: Religious Terror in Gothic Fiction', in G. R. Thompson (ed.), *The Gothic Imagination: Essays in Dark Romanticism* (Pullman, Washington, 1974), pp. 42–64.

Praz, M., *The Romantic Agony,* 2nd edn., trans. A. Davidson (London, 1951).

Price, M., 'The Picturesque Moment', in F. W. Hilles and H. Bloom (eds.), *From Sensibility to Romanticism: Essays Presented to Frederick A. Pottle* (New York, 1965), pp. 259–92.

Punter, D., *The Literature of Terror: A History of Gothic Fictions from 1765 to the Present Day* (London, 1980).

Radcliffe, Ann, *A Journey Made in the Summer of 1794, through Holland and the Western Frontier of Germany, With a Return Down the Rhine: To Which are added Observations During a Tour to the Lakes of Lancashire, Westmoreland, and Cumberland,* 2nd edn. (2 vols., London, 1796).

— *A Sicilian Romance,* new edn. (2 vols., London, 1821; repr. 2 vols. in 1, New York, 1972).

— *The Castles of Athlin and Dunbayne. A Highland Story,* new edn. (London, 1821; repr. New York, 1972).

— *The Italian or the Confessional of the Black Penitents: A Romance,* ed. F. Garber (London, 1968).

— *The Mysteries of Udolpho: A Romance,* ed. B. Dobrée (London, 1970).

— 'On the Supernatural in Poetry', *New Monthly Magazine,* xvi (1826), 145–52.

— *The Romance of the Forest*, new edn. (3 vols., London, 1827; repr. New York, 1974).

Radcliffe, Mary-Anne, *Manfroné; or, The One-Handed Monk. A Romance,* 3rd edn. (4 vols., London, 1828; repr. 4 vols. in 2, New York, 1972).

Railo, E., *The Haunted Castle: A Study of the Elements of English Romanticism* (London, 1927).

Raleigh, W., *The English Novel, Being a Short Sketch of its History from the Earliest Times to the Appearance of* Waverley (London, 1894).

Raysor, T. M. (ed.), *Coleridge's Miscellaneous Criticism* (London, 1936).

Reeve, Clara, *The Exiles; or, Memoirs of the Count de Cronstadt* (3 vols., London, 1788).

— *The Old English Baron: A Gothic Story,* ed. J. Trainer (London, 1967).

Review of John Bird, *The Castle of Hardayne; a Romance,* in the *Analytical Review,* xxiii (1796), 55.

Review of *The Castle of Mowbray. An English Romance* (By the Author of *St. Bernard's Priory*), in the *Critical Review,* lxvi (1788), 577.

Review of *The Castles of Athlin and Dunblayne [sic], an Highland Story*, in the *Critical Review*, lxviii (1789), 251.

Review of *Count Roderic's Castle; or, Gothic Times, a Tale*, in the *Analytical Review*, xx (1794), 488–9.

Review of M. G. Lewis, *Feudal Tyrants*, in the *Critical Review*, 3rd ser., xi (1807), 273–8.

Review of *Longsword Earl of Salisbury. An Historical Romance*, in the *Critical Review*, xiii (1762), 252–7.

Review of *Melmoth the Wanderer*, in the *Monthly Review*, 2nd ser., xciv (1821), 81–90.

Review of *Melmoth the Wanderer*, in the *Athenaeum*, no. 3366 (1892), pp. 560–1.

Review of *The Romance of the Forest*, in the *Critical Review*, 2nd ser., iv (1792), 458–60.

Rieger, H., '*Au pied de la lettre:* Stylistic Uncertainty in *Vathek*', *Criticism*, iv (1962), 302–12.

Roberts, B. B., *The Gothic Romance: Its Appeal to Women Writers and Readers in Late Eighteenth-century England* (New York, 1980).

Rollins, H. E. (ed.), *The Letters of John Keats 1814–1821* (2 vols., Cambridge, Mass., 1958).

Sade, D. A. F., Marquis de, *Idée sur les romans*, ed. O. Uzanne (Paris, 1878).

Sadleir, M., *The Northanger Novels: A Footnote to Jane Austen*, English Association Pamphlet no. 68 (November, 1927) (Oxford, 1927).

[Scott, Sir Walter], Introd. to *The Castle of Otranto; A Gothic Story* (Edinburgh, 1811).

—— 'Prefatory Memoir to Mrs Ann Radcliffe', in *The Novels of Mrs Ann Radcliffe*, Ballantyne's Novelist's Library, x (London, 1824), i–xxxix.

—— Review of Dennis Jasper Murphy (Charles Robert Maturin), *Fatal Revenge; or, the Family of Montorio: a Romance*, in the *Quarterly Review*, iii (1810), 339–47.

Sedgwick, E. K., 'The Character in the Veil: Imagery of the Surface in the Gothic Novel', *PMLA* xcvi (1981), 255–70.

Shelley, Percy Bysshe, *Zastrozzi: A Romance* (1810), in R. Ingpen and W. E. Peck (eds.), *The Complete Works of Percy Bysshe Shelley* (10 vols., London, 1926–30), v.

Shepperson, A. B., *The Novel in Motley: A History of the Burlesque Novel in English* (Cambridge, Mass., 1936).

Smith, N. C., 'Sense, Sensibility and Ann Radcliffe', *Studies in English Literature*, xiii (1973), 577–90.

Smith, W. H., 'Strawberry Hill and Otranto', *TLS* 23 May 1936, p. 440.

Solomon, S. J., 'Subverting Propriety as a Pattern of Irony in Three Eighteenth-century Novels: *The Castle of Otranto, Vathek,* and *Fanny Hill', Erasmus Review,* i (1971), 107–16.

Stephen, L., 'Horace Walpole', in *Hours in a Library,* new edn., with additions (4 vols., London, 1907), ii. 103–45.

Summers, M., *A Gothic Bibliography* (London, 1940; repr. New York, 1964).

—— *The Gothic Quest: A History of the Gothic Novel* (London, 1938; repr. New York, 1964).

Sypher, W., 'Social Ambiguity in a Gothic Novel', *Partisan Review,* xii (1945), 50–60.

[Talfourd, T. N.], 'Remarks on "Melmoth" ', *New Monthly Magazine, and Universal Register*, xiv. ii (1820), 662–8.

—— 'Memoir of the Life and Writings of Mrs Radcliffe', in *Gaston de Blondeville, or the Court of Henry III. Keeping Festival in Ardenne, A Romance.—St. Alban's Abbey, A Metrical Tale; With Some Poetical Pieces. By Anne Radcliffe* (4 vols., London, 1826), i. 3–132.

Tarr, M. M., *Catholicism in Gothic Fiction: A Study of the Nature and Function of Catholic Materials in Gothic Fiction in England* (Washington, DC, 1946).

Tatar, M. M., 'The Houses of Fiction: Toward a Definition of the Uncanny', *Comparative Literature,* xxxiii (1981), 167–82.

'Terrorist Novel Writing', *Spirit of the Public Journals,* i (1797), 227–9.

Thompson, G. R. (ed.), *The Gothic Imagination: Essays in Dark Romanticism* (Pullman, Washington, 1974).

Thorp, W., 'The Stage Adventures of Some Gothic Novels', *PMLA* xliii (1928), 476–86.

Thorslev, P. L., jun., *The Byronic Hero: Types and Prototypes* (Minneapolis, 1962).

Todorov, T., *The Fantastic: A Structural Approach to a Literary Genre,* trans. R. Howard (Cleveland, 1973).

Tompkins, J. M. S., *The Popular Novel in England 1770–1800* (London, 1932; repr. Lincoln, Nebraska, 1961).

Trostaniecki, I., 'La poétique du caché dans *Le Moine* de M. G. Lewis', *Recherches anglaises et américaines,* vi (1973), 43–59.

Varma, D. P., *The Gothic Flame, Being a History of the Gothic Novel in England: Its Origins, Efflorescence, Disintegration, and Residuary Influences* (London, 1957).

Walpole, Horace, 'Autograph Diary of Admission to Strawberry Hill, 1784–1796', MS WM 2.10, Houghton Library, Harvard University, Cambridge, Mass.

— *The Castle of Otranto: A Gothic Story,* ed. W. S. Lewis (London, 1969).

— *A Description of the Villa of Mr. Horace Walpole . . . at Strawberry-Hill near Twickenham . . .* (Strawberry Hill, 1784).

— *Hieroglyphic Tales,* with an introd. by K. W. Gross, Augustan Reprint Society Publication nos. 212–13 (Los Angeles, 1982).

— *Memoranda Walpoliana* (1761–1799), ed. and with an introd. by W. S. Lewis, Miscellaneous Antiquities, xiii (Farmington, Conn., 1937).

— *The Mysterious Mother* (Strawberry Hill, 1768).

— *Notes by Horace Walpole on Several Characters of Shakespeare,* ed. W. S. Lewis, Miscellaneous Antiquities, xvi (Farmington, Conn., 1940).

Ware, M., *Sublimity in the Novels of Ann Radcliffe: A Study of the Influence upon her Craft of Edmund Burke's 'Enquiry into the Origin of Our Ideas of the Sublime and Beautiful',* Essays and Studies on English Language and Literature, xxv (Upsala, 1963).

Watt, I., *The Rise of the Novel: Studies in Defoe, Richardson and Fielding* (Berkeley and Los Angeles, 1957).

Watt, W. W., *Shilling Shockers of the Gothic School: A Study of Chapbook Gothic Romances,* Harvard Honors Theses in English, v (Cambridge, Mass., 1932; repr. New York, 1967).

Weiskel, T., *The Romantic Sublime: Studies in the Structure and Psychology of Transcendence* (Baltimore, 1976).

Wilt, J., *Ghosts of the Gothic: Austen, Eliot, & Lawrence* (Princeton, NJ, 1980).

Woolf, Virginia, 'Across the Border', *TLS* 31 January 1918, p. 55; repr. as 'The Supernatural in Fiction' in *Granite and Rainbow* (London, 1958), pp. 61–4.

— 'Gothic Romance', *TLS* 5 May 1921, p. 288; repr. in *Granite and Rainbow* (London, 1958), pp. 57–60.

The Yale Edition of Horace Walpole's Correspondence, ed. W. S. Lewis *et al.* (48 vols., New Haven, 1937–83).

Index